THE ECONOMICS AND ETHICS OF LONG-TERM CARE AND DISABILITY

THE ECONOMICS AND ETHICS OF LONG-TERM CARE

CARE A·N·D

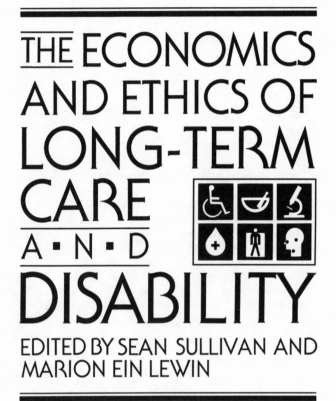

DISABILITY

EDITED BY SEAN SULLIVAN AND MARION EIN LEWIN

American Enterprise Institute for Public Policy Research
Washington, D.C.

Sean Sullivan is vice president of New Directions for Policy. Marion Ein Lewin is a senior staff officer and director of health policy fellowship programs at the Institute of Medicine, National Academy of Sciences.

Distributed by arrangement with
UPA, Inc.
4720 Boston Way
Lanham, MD 20706
3 Henrietta Street
London WC2E 8LU, England

Library of Congress Cataloging-in-Publication Data

The Economics and ethics of long-term care and disability / Sean
   Sullivan and Marion Ein Lewin, editors.
      p.   cm.   —   (AEI study ; 467)
   ISBN 0-8447-3645-7 (alk. paper). ISBN 0-8447-3646-5 (pbk. :   alk.
paper)
   1. Long-term care of the sick—United States.   2. Long-term care
of the sick—Government policy—United States.   I. Sullivan, Sean.
II. Lewin, Marion Ein.   III. American Enterprise Institute for
Public Policy Research.   IV. Series: AEI studies ;   467.
   RA644.6.E28   1988
   362.1'6'0973—dc19   87-30829
                                                                   CIP

1 3 5 7 9 10 8 6 4 2

AEI Studies 467

Printed in the United States of America

Acknowledgments

We thank the Pew Charitable Trust for its support of the seminars and research that made this book possible. We also extend our appreciation to the Pew health policy fellows who offered their constructive critiques of earlier drafts of the papers that make up the bulk of this book, including Bridget Simone, University of Michigan; Deborah Ward, Boston University; Helen H. Schauffler, Brandeis University; and Sharon Arnold, the Rand Corporation–University of California, Los Angeles.

SEAN SULLIVAN
MARION EIN LEWIN

Contents

Contributors

ARTHUR L. CAPLAN is director of the Center for Biomedical Ethics at the University of Minnesota. He is the former associate director of the Hastings Center, Institute of Society, Ethics, and the Life Sciences, where he wrote extensively on health policy, medical ethics, and ethical issues in science and technology.

MITCHELL P. LAPLANTE is an assistant research sociologist at the Institute for Health and Aging at the University of California, San Francisco. He has done research on the socioeconomic correlates of multiple chronic conditions and the competing risks of disease and disability.

SHELAH LEADER is a health policy analyst with the Public Policy Institute of the American Association of Retired Persons. She has published widely on policy issues affecting women, consumers, and the aged.

MARION EIN LEWIN is a senior staff officer and director of health policy fellowship programs at the Institute of Medicine, National Academy of Sciences, in Washington, D.C. She is the former director of the Center for Health Policy Research at the American Enterprise Institute.

JUDITH W. MELTZER is a senior research associate at the Center for the Study of Social Policy in Washington, D.C. She has worked extensively on projects in the areas of poverty, long-term care, health, and human services.

DOROTHY P. RICE is a professor at the Institute for Health and Aging at the University of California, San Francisco. From 1976 to 1982 she was director of the National Center for Health Statistics, where she led the development and management of a nationwide health care information system.

SEAN SULLIVAN is vice president of New Directions for Policy, a social policy research consulting firm in Washington, D.C. He is a former senior policy analyst at the Center for Health Policy Research at the American Enterprise Institute.

IRVING KENNETH ZOLA is professor of sociology at Brandeis University in Waltham, Massachusetts. He is also cofounder of the Boston Self-Help Center, a counseling, advocacy, resource, and education center devoted to and staffed primarily by people with chronic disabilities.

1
Introduction and Overview

Sean Sullivan and Marion Ein Lewin

The changing dynamics of the health care marketplace and the growth of competitive forces have been well chronicled in recent years. Not so well publicized, however, has been a more gradual but no less profound change that has been under way for a good while now—the emergence of chronic conditions and disabilities as the major health problems of the latter twentieth century.

To some extent, the supplanting of acute disease as our largest health care problem is a result of the success of our medical enterprise. Improved diagnosis and treatment of acute conditions have been the story of medical progress for most of this century, with results that can be seen in reduced mortality and longer life expectancies. The curative, medically based health care system that has grown up in response to acute diseases, however, is not so well suited to dealing with the different problem of chronic disease and disability.

The essays in this volume suggest that the health care system should be reoriented to deal with functional disability, which does not lend itself so readily to being "cured" but, rather, often needs to be "managed." The aim in treating chronic illnesses or disabilities is often very different: to enable the individual to function with the greatest degree of independence attainable in performing the essential activities of daily living. In other words, the objective should be to allow persons with these conditions to remain full participants in the life of our society.

A reoriented system would be more unified, combining or coordinating health and social services that are usually kept in separate compartments and administered by different entities. The medical model concerns itself almost exclusively with health care, which meets only some of the needs of individuals trying to maintain themselves either at home or in a work setting. Other kinds of services, such as help with certain daily activities or with transportation, are often the most critical needs of those with disabling conditions; a new

1

model that includes these services as well as traditional health care must be developed to replace the old medical one.

Reorienting the system will require more than simply merging health and social services to meet a wider range of needs in an effective manner. The roles of the principal actors in the system—of providers and consumers—must also change. Under the medical model, patients depend almost completely on physicians to decide for them what services they need and how those services will be provided. Individuals being treated for acute conditions have been willing to surrender their autonomy in part because they expect to regain it fully after they are cured. Individuals with chronic or disabling conditions face a different situation. They may have to live with these conditions indefinitely and are not so willing to put their lives under the control of medical professionals. Like the elderly, they seek to maintain their autonomy—and may view physicians as a threat to it.

Giving consumers of health care more autonomy has major implications for the training of health professionals, as well as for the greater use of ancillary and nonmedical service providers. Physicians need to view persons with chronic or disabling conditions less as patients over whom they exercise strict and somewhat impersonal control and more as individuals who need to be informed about treatment procedures and effects. In short, they need to treat them like consumers of other products and services. To shape a delivery system more responsive to the needs of the chronically ill, medical providers may also have to yield more of the "market" to those who can deliver the range of relatively "low-tech" services needed by persons with functional impairments.

Perhaps the nature of the changes needed in the system of care and assistance for the chronically ill and disabled is best described by one of the authors in this volume, when he calls for a commitment to "equal opportunity" for these individuals to pursue their lives and careers by mitigating the effects of their impairments. The public and private sectors have complementary roles to play in ensuring such opportunities. Public policies can be reshaped much further to provide financial support for services and providers that have not come within the boundaries of the traditional medical model. And private employers can redesign jobs and provide support services of their own so that more persons with limited functional impairments can find employment and thereby be self-sustaining.

Each chapter of this volume speaks to some aspects of this overarching theme of changing public policies and our health care system to address the issues raised by chronic illness and disability. Dorothy

Rice and Mitchell LaPlante describe the increasing prevalence of disabling conditions in our society, highlighting the importance of the subject. Judy Meltzer argues the need for improving existing public programs until a new financing strategy and greater private initiative can be achieved. Arthur Caplan and Irving Zola, between them, provide a comprehensive critique of the current medical approach to dealing with long-term functional impairment and describe the elements of a new public policy approach. Finally, Shelah Leader examines the disproportionate impact of inadequate long-term care programs on women, who make up most of the nursing home population.

Dorothy Rice and Mitchell LaPlante present findings on the increasing extent of chronic illness and disability in the United States. They describe trends in mortality and life expectancy and examine the extent to which chronic conditions cause disabilities and limitations on the ability to work and perform other major life activities. They found that nearly 33 million Americans, or 14 percent of the noninstitutionalized population, were disabled—that is, limited in their activity by chronic conditions—in 1985. More than one-fourth of them, 9 million people, were unable to carry on their major activity.

Life expectancy has risen notably in the latter half of this century, and the rate of decline in mortality has accelerated sharply in the past twenty years. At the same time, Rice and LaPlante found that the prevalence of chronic conditions that limit activity increased more than one-fifth during the 1970s for the noninstitutionalized population. The greatest increase, perhaps surprisingly, occurred for the under-seventeen age group, which the authors attribute largely to changing perceptions of what constitutes illness, to reflect the "new morbidity" of childhood conditions with a larger psychosocial component.

Although disability is often associated with older persons, Rice and LaPlante found that the group with the next largest increase in prevalence of disabling conditions was the working population aged forty-five to sixty-four. Much of this increase they attribute to reduced mortality, which results in prolonging disabilities. Another cause may be the availability of more generous social insurance programs than in the past.

Rice and LaPlante found that the prevalence of disabling conditions actually declined for the noninstitutionalized population seventy-five and older, perhaps because the healthier elderly are remaining in the community while the frailer are entering nursing homes. All age groups report more multiple disabling conditions and re-

3

stricted activity days related to them; the authors attribute the increase to greater awareness stimulated by increased access to medical
services, as well as to higher survival rates for the disabled.

The only possibility Rice and LaPlante see for reversing the trend
toward greater prevalence of disabilities would be to postpone them
to later years, reducing the incidence in younger age groups through
enhanced primary prevention efforts. Otherwise, increasing numbers
of chronically ill and disabled across age groups will require more
rehabilitation, income support, and long-term care to maintain their
economic status and functional independence. Yet interpretation of
eligibility rules for public programs has been tightened, making it
more difficult for many to qualify for Social Security Disability Insurance and Supplemental Security Income benefits.

Judy Meltzer's chapter, "Financing Long-Term Care: A Major
Obstacle to Reform," speaks to the issue of how to meet more effectively the chronic, long-term care requirements of tomorrow's elderly
and disabled. Recent expansion of Medicare to pay for the catastrophic costs associated with lengthy acute hospital stays has served
to illuminate what many observers consider to be the most critical gap
in existing health care coverage. Meltzer provides us with an extremely useful synthesis of the current long-term care debate, describing those areas where consensus appears to exist as well as
pointing to those unresolved issues that need further attention and
research.

Meltzer finds, for example, an emerging consensus that an effective and humane long-term care system must move away from past
overemphasis on the medical model and institutionalization and rely
more on community- and home-based services, using case management to control utilization and costs. The major challenge here, of
course, is how to finance such a revised structure of care giving,
especially with the significant contribution now provided by informal
networks and family members.

A question often raised in current calls for reform is to what
degree to combine separate financing for acute and long-term care.
There appears to be growing support for better integration and wider
application of delivery models such as social/health maintenance organizations (social/HMOs), which provide integrated financing and
delivery of acute care, institutional chronic care, and community-
based social support. A related aspect is whether programs for the
elderly and the disabled, groups that share certain basic problems but
may have different needs, should be unified. Meltzer also discusses
some of the pros and cons of financing chronic care through vouchers
and income supplements versus additional payments to providers.

4

Finally, the author asks whether limited public resources can best be allocated on the basis of functional impairment or of financial need.

While Meltzer foresees the necessity of a major federal role in the financing of future long-term care, she underscores the importance of encouraging workable public-private partnerships as well. A special challenge here is to develop innovative financing options targeted to middle-income citizens, a group that now finds itself caught in the all-or-nothing dilemma of having to pay for long-term care services almost completely out-of-pocket or spend down to impoverishment and Medicaid eligibility. A number of states are fashioning programs to encourage this target population to purchase private long-term care insurance with the promise that, when benefits under such coverage are used up, policy holders can become eligible for Medicaid without the spend-down requirement.

Arthur Caplan argues that the issues raised by chronic illness and disability require ethical rather than economic analysis for their resolution. Our society gives no special ethical status to chronic illness, tending to view all disease as a single category. Caplan argues that chronic conditions are different in kind from acute illness and require different responses from patients, providers, and policy makers. Chronic illness and disability do not fit the prevailing medical model for diagnosing and treating acute disease and are not favored by third-party payers precisely because they do not fit this model, even while they are not given a separate and legitimate status of their own. Caplan believes that it is the fear of a massive reallocation of resources away from acute care that has kept chronic conditions from gaining this legitimacy.

According to Caplan, prevailing ethical theories posit a duty of beneficence in our society when several conditions are met: there is a clear and serious need, aid can be given to alleviate the need, there are no reasonable alternative sources of aid, and providing assistance will not create undue burdens or risks. He suggests that chronic conditions do not meet these criteria as well as acute conditions: needs are often less palpable, less responsive to treatments, able to be met by people who are not medical professionals, and likelier to impose financial and other burdens on those giving aid.

Caplan believes that many of the problems experienced by the chronically ill and the disabled are as much social as medical. They do not want to surrender their autonomy to medical professionals as the acutely ill have done; yet they find that they must conform somewhat to the medical model to legitimate their conditions in the eyes of society, which still expects them to function independently. Broadening the medical model to include them might gain a larger share of

5

medical resources but at the cost of categorizing them as permanent wards of society instead of as autonomous persons. Caplan would make them conceptually distinct to confer on them a different status, as people seeking equal social opportunity to lead their own lives rather than beneficence or charity. Shifting the emphasis from beneficence to opportunity means, to Caplan, that public policy for the chronically ill and disabled should be less concerned with health care and more with social services.

Irving Zola issues a call for a unified health policy agenda concerning the aging and the disabled, made more urgent by the projected increase in the prevalence of chronic and disabling conditions even as mortality declines and life expectancy increases. Zola points out that disabilities will be present for more of a person's life span in the future and will change in nature over time. For example, infant mortality has declined in part because advances in neonatology enable more infants to survive but often with some kind of impairment. Greater fitness at middle age will "compress" morbidity toward the end of the life span, he predicts, but an aging population will put more people at risk for conditions that limit their activity.

Zola takes issue with the technicalization of health care, which he sees leading to an "objectification" of care and of those who give and receive it. He questions our faith in the technological fix, which implies that all problems have technical solutions and that passive patients can do little to deal with their own problems. This faith encourages "objective" measurement of outcomes, such as the quantity of tasks that can be performed without help, rather than the quality of life that can be lived *with* some help. And Zola argues that the technical focus of medical education is creating a distance between care givers and recipients that gets in the way of dealing with chronic illness.

The process of medicalization has expanded medical influence into areas of care where its effects may be harmful, according to Zola. He believes that medicine has joined law and religion as a major institution of social control and arbiter of social values in America. Zola asserts that calling a problem "medical" gives doctors control of it and forecloses other social interventions while also obscuring the moral issues raised by what he terms the "reification" of medical measurement. He sees measurement as a tool and not an answer to decisions that he believes are ultimately moral and political rather than scientific.

Zola views the movement toward providing services at home as a reaction against both the technicalization and the medicalization of care, citing a lack of evidence that more spending on health care results in better health. But he points out, ironically, that technology is making the home more like the hospital room, tending to defeat the purpose of the shift. Zola sets out two models for delivering services to this population: (1) the home health–medical model, aimed at meeting posthospital acute care needs, leaving accountability with the provider and funding tied to the health care system; (2) the contrasting attendant care–independent living model, aimed at meeting continuing chronic care needs, making the consumer accountable and seeking funding from the larger social services system.

To produce a unified policy agenda, Zola calls for a change in the identity of, and the perspective on, those with chronic conditions and disabilities. The medical model has categorized them as physiologically inferior and vulnerable and has separated them into various clinical entities. This model is being questioned both inside and outside the medical profession, as chronic conditions are being seen as multicausal and complex, with many commonalities. To regain their autonomy from medical professionals, Zola argues, patients must separate themselves from their conditions and realize that they have multiple identities, that they are not their diseases. If different groups of disabled persons perceive their common needs, they can work together for service orientations and design technologies that will help them overcome their limitations. A more universal concept of need should remove the stigma felt by many of the disabled, even as more socially oriented services give them back the control of their lives that has been ceded to technical and professional medical providers.

Shelah Leader takes a critical look at the design flaws in Medicare from the perspective of older women, who are exposed to greater financial liability and spend more of their incomes on health care than men do. Nearly a quarter of the eighty-five-and-older population lives in nursing homes, and more than two-thirds of this population is female. These "old" elderly are almost twice as likely as the sixty-five to seventy-four age group to be poor or near-poor. Leader argues that Medicare's failure to cover the cost of chronic care services provided at home or, except under very limited circumstances, in nursing care facilities pauperizes women more often, since they make up the great majority of those elderly who end up in nursing homes and, eventually, on Medicaid. The demographic trend toward an older, increasingly female population at greater risk of needing chronic care worsens the effects of this lack of coverage for long-term care services.

Leader does not believe that many of the elderly can afford to enroll in available social/HMOs or life-care communities, nor does she think that medical individual retirement accounts (IRAs) or private insurance for long-term care will meet the needs of most older people. She argues for more publicly funded financial protection against catastrophic health care costs but acknowledges that this is not likely to occur soon in the face of current and projected federal budget deficits.

The chapters in this volume call for changing the terms of health care and the structure of care giving in our society. Mounting serious efforts in this direction appears today to be especially relevant and timely. The changing demographic profile of our nation suggests that the number of people with conditions that interfere with their full social participation will steadily increase. Our past emphasis on and faith in technological solutions need to be reexamined in light of growing health care needs that do not fit neatly into the traditional medical model. These essays are meant to offer fresh insights into the changing nature of our health care needs, as well as practical suggestions about how to start moving away from the medical model in the new direction they point out.

2
Chronic Illness, Disability, and Increasing Longevity

Dorothy P. Rice and Mitchell P. LaPlante

As mortality rates have declined and people are living longer to ages at which the risks of chronic illness and disability are high, the question whether the health of the nation is improving is one of pivotal importance for society. The problem has two dimensions with vastly different implications. On the one hand, people may live to older ages increasingly free of chronic disease and impairment. The burden of chronic conditions on society will then decline over time. Such a pattern could be a result of effective disease prevention and health promotion. On the other hand, people with chronic diseases and impairments may live longer without being cured of their conditions. Medical intervention may effectively control acute life-threatening episodes without eliminating the disability due to chronic conditions. Then the burden on society will increase as people survive longer in a disabled state, creating even greater need for medical and social services.

The two dimensions can vary independently; incidence rates (the rate of new cases) of chronic conditions can decline while the rate of survival of persons with chronic conditions increases. The effect of the trends will depend on the relative magnitudes of change; they may offset each other, producing over the short term no net change in the prevalence rate (the rate of existing conditions, including new cases) of chronic conditions. Inevitably, however, a continued decline in incidence will eventually lead to a decline in prevalence. The worst prospect is that both the incidence rates of chronic conditions and survival rates may increase without curing conditions, a situation that would cause the prevalence rates of chronic diseases and impairments to increase dramatically.

This chapter explores the relationships among chronic illness, impairment, disability, and increasing longevity. Because disability

9

has more profound consequences than chronic conditions in general, we focus on trends in the prevalence of disability and the frequency with which the disabled used medical services in the period from 1969 to 1981. We also examine trends in the prevalence rates of multiple chronic disabling conditions, to provide additional insight into trends in disability.

Considerable attention has been focused on improvements in the health of the nation as shown by declining mortality rates and increasing longevity. As longevity has increased, however, chronic conditions occurring in middle and old age have emerged as major causes of disability and functional dependency, accounting for a large proportion of the nation's expenditures for health care. The problems associated with these conditions have profound implications for individuals, families, and society. For the individual they may mean pain and suffering, financial strain, disability, dependence, and deterioration in the quality of life. Families of victims and those who render care may be forced to change their life styles and forgo job opportunities. The costs to society are substantial in lost productivity and expenditures for medical and other care. Conjecture and controversy arise, however, over future morbidity patterns, as we observe that declining mortality rates have been accompanied by increasing morbidity and limitations of activity due to chronic conditions for middle-aged and older people and rising work disability rates over the past two decades.

This chapter is organized as follows:

- It presents summary highlights of our findings.
- It defines disease, illness, impairment, and disability and discusses their relationship to mortality as a basis for understanding the temporal relationships among mortality and other indicators of health status.
- It reviews trends in life expectancy and mortality, the effects of declining mortality on the demographic structure of the population, and its implications for future needs for long-term care in an aging society that may be at risk of chronic illness, disability, and functional dependency.
- It presents comparative data on the magnitude of disability in the United States.
- It discusses recent studies of trends in chronic illness and disability.
- It analyzes trends in multiple chronic conditions causing limitations of major life activities over the period 1969–1971 to 1979–1981.

Summary Highlights

The principal goals of this chapter are to establish the magnitude and patterns of the prevalence of chronic illness and disability among different age groups and to examine how these patterns have changed in the context of declining mortality rates and increasing longevity. To describe mortality and life expectancy trends, we used vital and health statistics data; for the analysis of trends in morbidity, disability, and medical care utilization, we used data from the continuing National Health Interview Survey (NHIS) over two periods: 1969 to 1971 and 1979 to 1981. The NHIS is a nationwide sample survey in which data are collected through household interviews on personal and demographic characteristics, illnesses, injuries, impairments, chronic conditions, limitations of major activity and work, health insurance coverage, and other health topics.

The highlights of our findings are as follows:

• Improvements in life expectancy since the middle of the twentieth century are notable even though there are significant current differences between men and women and between black and white persons, with women living longest.
• There has been a marked acceleration since the late 1960s in the rate of decline in mortality rates across all age ranges and for many chronic diseases, including heart disease and stroke, two of the three leading causes of death in the United States. Death rates are expected to continue to decline in the future as further advances are made against degenerative diseases.
• The demographic structure of the nation has shifted to an older population. The elderly have risen rapidly both in numbers and as a proportion of the total population. One in five Americans will be elderly by the year 2030, compared with one in nine in 1980. The fastest-growing segment of the population is the very old, who are at high risk of chronic illness, functional dependency, disability, and institutionalization.
• There is no direct relationship between the leading causes of death and the prevalence of chronic disease. Among the most prevalent chronic conditions are sinusitis, arthritis, and impairments; the last two are often highly disabling but are seldom fatal.
• Persons who suffer from chronic disabling conditions are more restricted in their daily activities, are much more likely to need the help of another person in performing basic activities, and are higher users of medical resources than persons not disabled by chronic conditions. Almost half—47 percent—of disabled persons who

11

need the help of another person or a device in performing basic activities of daily living are under age sixty-five.

• When disability is defined in terms of any limitation of activity by chronic conditions, the number of noninstitutionalized disabled persons in 1985 was 32.7 million, or 14 percent of the total population. More than one-fourth, or 9 million persons, are unable to carry on their major activity.

• About 4.4 million disabled persons of working age (eighteen to sixty-four) currently receive benefits under the Social Security Disability Insurance (SSDI) or the Supplemental Security Income (SSI) programs, but at least 3.3 million persons who are unable to work because of health problems do not receive federal disability benefits. For those without financial assistance, disability undoubtedly causes severe disruptions in economic resources and family life. Financing medical care services for persons who are disabled but do not receive Medicaid or Medicare benefits is an important legislative priority.

• Over the period 1969–1971 to 1979–1981, the prevalence rate of limitations in activity increased significantly, indicating worsening health. It increased more than one-fifth for the entire noninstitutionalized population, with greater increases for women than for men. The greatest increases occurred for children and youth and for middle-aged persons, forty-five to sixty-four years old, especially for the most disabled—those unable to carry on their major activity. The prevalence rate of limitation declined slightly in later years (ages seventy-five and over), indicating perhaps that the health of the very old living in the community has improved slightly. But comparison of health indicators over time for the very old must control for changes in institutionalization, which are not addressed here.

• Disabled people reported more chronic conditions and more days of restricted activity over this period. The number of chronic conditions per person causing limitation of activity increased 12.5 percent, with increases reported for all ages and the greatest increase for those aged eighty-five years and over, suggesting worsening health. In general, the more severely disabled population reported the greatest increases in multiple chronic conditions, which suggests that persons may be living longer with severely disabling chronic conditions.

• While days of restricted activity per disabled person increased between the two periods, bed disability days remained relatively constant. Days of restricted activity per person increased most for those who were unable to perform their major activity and reported three or more disabling chronic conditions. On the average these persons experienced almost three weeks more of restricted activity in 1979–1981 than in 1969–1971.

• Physicians' visits per disabled person remained constant, while hospital days of care declined by 14 percent. These data reflect overall trends toward limiting the length of stay in hospitals.

• Under conditions of declining mortality, increases in the prevalence of disability, the number of disabling conditions, and greater restriction of activity among the severely disabled suggest that people may be more disabled as they live longer. The oldest old may be an exception, but trend data on institutional placement are needed to verify this possibility.

Concepts of Disease, Illness, and Disability

The terms "illness," "sickness," "impairment," "disability," and "handicap" are used with a great deal of inconsistency. A number of attempts to clarify the terms have been made, the most notable among them the recommendations of the World Health Organization (WHO) for international use.[1] We draw heavily in this discussion on the WHO recommendations. The relationships of the terms to be discussed are shown in figure 2–1.

Disease is defined as any bodily disturbance associated with a characteristic set of signs or symptoms. Signs consist of observable health characteristics such as fever, lumps, elevated blood pressure, and laboratory results. Symptoms, however, are not directly observable but are reported by individuals. They consist of changes in feel-

FIGURE 2–1

MODEL OF ILLNESS CONCEPTS

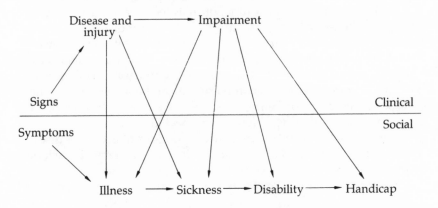

13

ings, such as increased pain or weakness, reduced endurance, or other perceived changes.

Injury refers to damage inflicted on a body by some traumatic, usually external, force. Both disease and injury are manifest by signs and symptoms; the distinction between them is one of putative cause. Diagnoses of disease or injury are seldom made on the basis of symptoms alone; medical providers are guided by symptoms to look for signs that increase the probability that a diagnosis (or a set of diagnoses) is correct. The concepts of disease and injury are clinical ones; different terms are necessary to describe the experiences of individuals.

Illness is the perception of disease or injury by the individual, more often by the experience of symptoms than by attention to signs. Illness is a psychological state; a person may feel ill in the absence of clinically verified disease or injury.

Sickness, the state of being labeled by oneself or others as having a disease or injury, is a sociological state with attending rights and obligations. In Western societies it is incumbent on persons adopting the sick role to seek medical attention and attempt to get well in exchange for certain exemptions from usual social activity, such as attending work or school. Not all illness leads to sickness; people may feel ill without allowing their illness to disrupt their usual activity.

Disease, injury, and illness are usually classified as *acute* or *chronic* according to the length of time a person has been affected. A common measure of "chronic" in population surveys is a duration of three or more months.

Impairment is a chronic physiological, psychological, or anatomical abnormality of bodily structure or function caused by disease or injury. Physiological and anatomical function may be measured by such variables as blood pressure, cardiovascular function, and bone density or by specific movements such as walking, running, or lifting heavy objects. Psychological function may be measured by anxiety, stress, or intellectual and reasoning abilities. Abnormalities of anatomical structure may include loss, absence, or disfigurement. By this definition disease and injury do not necessarily imply impairment, but impairment does imply that disease or injury must be or must have been present. A chronic impairment can be a result of arrested disease processes, prior injury, or congenital anomaly. In such cases a person with an impairment may neither feel ill nor act sick.

Chronic illness means the presence of long-term disease or disease symptoms. The term *chronic condition* is more general; it includes impairments not due to disease.

From the definitions above determining the existence of a chronic condition can be complicated. Assessments may depend on whether the affected person, another respondent, or a medical provider is asked and in what context. A person may be unaware of the existence of clinically observable signs of disease or injury and may therefore not report them. He or she may also deny the existence of clinically determined disease or injury or may feel ill and act sick in the absence of clinically observable signs of disease or injury. Sometimes a patient who does not feel ill may be told by a medical provider that he or she has a disease or injury and encouraged to adopt the sick role. We will comment later on the problem of divergence between reports of chronic conditions by patients and by providers.

When impairment interferes with normal activity over the long term, a person is said to have a disability. *Disability* is defined as "any restriction or lack (resulting from an impairment) of ability to perform an activity in the manner, or in the range, considered normal."[2] Since human activity is variable, there are many different kinds of disability. Population surveys often class disabilities by the degree of disruption of life's major activities. "Major activities" are usual or predominant roles that vary with age, such as going to school, performing work at a job or business, or doing housework. A distinction is often made between inability to perform one's major activity and limitations in the kind or amount of major activity a person can perform.

Categories of disability also include limitations in other activities: leisure activities, such as recreational sports; activities of daily living, such as eating, dressing, bathing, and toileting; and instrumental activities of daily living, including shopping, household chores, preparing meals, managing finances, and using the telephone.[3] Work limitations are a prime concern for adults up to the age of retirement, while the ability to live in the community with or without personal assistance in daily living is of prime concern for the frail elderly and others with severe physical, mental, or emotional impairments.

One kind of disability does not automatically imply another. Not everyone with a work disability requires assistance with personal care, nor are all persons who need such assistance limited in their work. The same kinds and degrees of physical or mental impairment can often lead to varying kinds and degrees of disability. Paralysis of an upper limb, to use Saad Z. Nagi's example, would disable a surgeon but perhaps not a schoolteacher or a student.[4]

Work disability is a function of the vocation for which a person is trained, which is often selected early in adulthood (and may be influenced by impairment existing in youth). The development or worsening of impairment may make it difficult to fulfill the physical, mental, and emotional requirements of a vocation already selected. If impairment motivates a change of occupation, the alternatives available will depend in part on the transferability of the skills a person possesses. Cognitive skills may compensate for physical impairments. Thus, while the surgeon may no longer be able to practice surgery, he or she could probably find employment. Transferability of skills and the occupational alternatives available may make the difference between being limited in the kind of work one can do and not being able to work at all.

It is important to distinguish these definitions of work disability from the statutory definition in the United States. The largest public sources of assistance to the disabled are the SSDI and SSI programs of the Social Security Administration, which employ the same definition of disability.

The SSDI program was established in 1956 to provide benefits only for the most severely disabled workers under age sixty-five. In addition to meeting the requirement of five years of work within ten years of the onset of disability, a beneficiary must be unable to engage in any substantial gainful activity because of a medically determinable physical or mental impairment that can be expected to last for a continuous period of not less than twelve months. The impairment must be so severe that the person is unable to engage in any gainful work in the national economy, regardless of whether such work exists in the immediate area in which the disabled person lives, whether a job vacancy exists, or whether the person would be hired for such a job. Since 1973 SSI has provided the severely disabled with cash assistance based on financial need, regardless of work experience. Disability is usually determined under both programs by the state vocational rehabilitation agencies. The statutory definition of disability is thus much more restrictive than the definition given above.

Handicap is the social and economic disadvantage that may result from impairment or disability and may entail loss of income, social status, or social contacts. A person with a severe work disability is more likely to be poor (38 percent of the disabled and only 10 percent of the nondisabled aged eighteen to sixty-four were at or below the poverty line in 1978) and more likely to be living alone (18 percent of the disabled and only 11 percent of the nondisabled lived alone in 1978).[5] Not all handicaps result from disability; a handicap may be due to an impairment that does not cause disability, such as facial disfigurement that may be a disadvantage in interpersonal relations.

Relations among Mortality, Impairment, and Disability

Mortality rates decline because people survive longer with a disease or fewer people develop disease or both. In the past, when mortality was caused largely by acute infectious disease, increasing life expectancy resulted in a greater number of years of active life. Improvements in living standards and nutrition meant that fewer people developed acute illnesses, especially those that were more often fatal at the younger ages. As mortality becomes dominated by chronic disease, however, increasing life expectancy—especially at the middle and later years—does not necessarily mean more active years, since delaying death can increase the numbers of persons with impairments and disabilities in the population.

The temporal links among mortality, impairment, and disability are complex and often indirect. Some of the most prevalent disabling conditions, such as arthritis and other musculoskeletal impairments, are seldom fatal, and their dynamics may be quite different from those of mortality. Indeed, less than half the disabled population report "fatal" diseases as a main or secondary cause of their disability.[6] Even if the incidence of fatal diseases declines, the prevalence of disability may increase because of the increasing risks of musculoskeletal and cognitive impairment as people age.

Mortality and disability also differ in that not all disability is due to disease, whether fatal or not. People suffer disabling impairments as aftereffects of violence and accidents. Of course, impairments may be a result of arrested disease processes, such as surgical amputation to combat cancer. Finally, people do not always die from the diseases they suffer. The recorded causes of death are the immediate causes and may not include all the diseases that afflicted the deceased or even those that caused the greatest disability. No single model of human mortality and aging adequately explains the link of mortality with chronic disease and disability.[7]

Because people are living longer, they may be at greater risk of developing chronic disabling conditions, the determinants of which may be quite different from those responsible for improving longevity. If people with chronic disabling conditions are surviving longer, we can expect the ranks of people with disability to swell. If the incidence of chronic disabling conditions is declining, however, the prevalence of disability may decline. New cases of disability may decline, perhaps because of changing life styles among younger age groups, while those with disabilities survive longer because of improved control of the progression of their conditions. Recent breakthroughs in medical technology have contributed to significant improvements in management and control of specific chronic diseases and perhaps to increases in life expectancy. Better access to increasingly more effective rehabilitation services would also reduce the prevalence of disability. Furthermore, changes in the social and physical environment significantly influence trends in disability. The conflu-

17

TABLE 2–1
LIFE EXPECTANCY AT BIRTH AND AT SIXTY-FIVE YEARS OF AGE, BY SEX AND RACE, UNITED STATES, 1900–1985
(years)

	Total	Males	Females	Whites	Blacks
At birth					
1900	47.3	46.3	48.3	47.6	33.0
1950	68.2	65.6	71.1	69.1	60.7
1960	69.7	66.6	73.1	70.6	63.2
1970	70.9	67.1	74.8	71.7	64.1
1980	73.7	70.0	77.4	74.4	68.1
1985a	74.7	71.2	78.2	75.3	69.5
At age 65					
1900	11.9	11.5	12.2	n.a.	n.a.
1950	13.9	12.8	15.0	n.a.	n.a.
1960	14.3	12.8	15.8	14.4	13.9
1970	15.2	13.1	17.0	15.2	14.2
1980	16.4	14.1	18.3	16.5	15.1
1985a	16.8	14.6	18.6	16.8	15.5

n.a. = not available.
a. Provisional data.
SOURCE: U.S. National Center for Health Statistics, *Health, United States, 1986*, table 12.

ence of these factors makes the relationship between trends in mortality and in disability quite indirect.

Life Expectancy

Life expectancy is a summary measure of the mortality profile of a population. Life expectancy and the death rates from which it is calculated are the oldest measures of health status. During the nineteenth and particularly the twentieth centuries, life expectancy has increased strikingly. Improvements in life expectancy earlier in this century reflected primarily reductions in infant mortality through the control of acute infectious diseases. More recent improvements have been due to declining mortality from chronic diseases at the middle and older ages.

Since 1950 six and one-half years have been added to life expectancy at birth and almost three years at age sixty-five (table 2–1). People born in 1950 could expect to live an average of 68.2 years; by 1985 life expectancy at birth had reached 74.7 years. In 1950 a person surviving to age sixty-five could expect to live 13.9 more years; by 1985 life expectancy at sixty-five had increased to 16.8 years.

Although improvements in life expectancy have been shared by males and females and by white and black persons, women and black persons have experienced the most rapid improvements. Between 1950 and 1985 women gained 7.1 years and men only 5.6 years; white persons gained 6.2 years and blacks 8.8 years. The differences in life expectancy at birth between men and women and between black and white persons are large. The difference for males and females widened gradually by almost a year, on the average, for each decade between 1950 and 1970; since 1970 it has declined.[8] It is too early, however, to forecast a trend toward further reduction of sex differences in life expectancy.

Mortality

In 1984 some 2.05 million persons died in the United States, a rate of 8.7 per 1,000 population.[9] Because the population has been aging, a more accurate picture of mortality trends is provided by the age-adjusted death rate, which, like life expectancy, eliminates the distortion associated with changing age composition. While the crude death rate for the total population declined 11 percent, the age-adjusted death rate declined 35 percent between 1950 and 1984 (table 2–2). Analysis shows two distinct periods: a moderate decline of 15 percent from 1950 to 1970 and a more rapid decline of 24 percent from 1970 to 1984.

Trends in mortality rates differ among age groups. Infant mortality rates decreased 67 percent between 1950 and 1984, the largest decline for any age group. Among young people fifteen to twenty-four years of age, death rates decreased 17 percent from 1950 to 1960, then increased at almost the same rate during the next ten years, and from 1970 to 1984 declined again by a dramatic 24 percent. Mortality rates for each of the ten-year age groups twenty-five to sixty-four years decreased about 12 to 14 percent from 1950 to 1970 and a striking 23 to 36 percent from 1970 to 1984. Similarly, mortality rates for the ten-year age groups sixty-five years and older decreased 12 to 13 percent from 1950 to 1970 and 13 to 21 percent from 1970 to 1984. This marked acceleration in the decline of mortality rates across all age ranges has had a significant effect on the demographic structure of the population and is the basis for population projections of an increasingly older age distribution.

Heart disease, a major chronic illness, is the leading cause of death in the United States and hence the predominant influence on

TABLE 2–2

CHANGE IN DEATH RATES, BY AGE, UNITED STATES, 1950–1984

(percent)

Age Group	1950–1984	1950–1970	1970–1984
All ages			
Age-adjusted death rate	− 35.1	− 15.1	− 23.6
Crude death rate	− 10.5	− 1.9	− 8.8
Under 1	− 67.1	− 35.1	− 49.3
1–4	− 62.8	− 39.4	− 38.6
5–14	− 55.6	− 31.3	− 46.6
15–24	− 24.4	− 0.3	− 24.2
25–34	− 32.2	− 11.9	− 23.1
35–44	− 42.9	− 12.3	− 35.8
45–54	− 39.0	− 14.5	− 28.6
55–64	− 32.6	− 13.2	− 22.4
65–74	− 30.0	− 11.9	− 20.5
75–84	− 31.4	− 14.2	− 20.1
85 and over	− 24.6	− 13.2	− 13.2

SOURCE: U.S. National Center for Health Statistics, *Health, United States, 1986*, table 20.

trends in total mortality. The age-adjusted death rate for heart disease decreased 40 percent from 1950 to 1984 (table 2–3). Suggested explanations for the decline include decreased smoking, improved management of hypertension, more healthful life styles, decreased dietary intake of saturated fats, more widespread physical activity, improved medical emergency services, and more widespread use and increased efficacy of coronary care units.

Malignant neoplasms, or cancers, are the second leading cause of death in the United States. The age-adjusted death rate for cancer has increased 6.5 percent since 1950. Cancer mortality has been increasing for some sites, including the respiratory system, breast, colon, pancreas, and bladder, and decreasing for others, including the stomach, rectum, cervix, and uterus. The highest rate of increase—200 percent since 1950—occurred in cancer of the respiratory system, attributable mainly to the effects of smoking.

Cerebrovascular disease, or stroke, is the third leading cause of death in the United States. The age-adjusted mortality rate for stroke decreased 25 percent from 1950 to 1970 and 50 percent from 1970 to 1984. Reductions were observed for men and women and for white and black people. Reasons for the recent decline include expanded hypertension screening programs, improved management and rehabilitation of stroke victims, and improved management of hypertension.

Three of the next seven leading causes of death in the United States are also chronic conditions: chronic obstructive pulmonary diseases, chronic liver disease and cirrhosis, and diabetes mellitus. Death rates increased 34 percent for chronic obstructive pulmonary diseases between 1970 and 1984 while rates for the two others declined approximately 30 percent. The ten leading causes of death include a few acute diseases (pneumonia and influenza) and external causes (accidents, suicide, and homicide).

Table 2–4 compares the ten leading causes of death in 1984 with the ten most prevalent chronic conditions in 1985 as reported in the National Health Interview Survey.[10] Heart disease, the leading cause of death, ranks only seventh in prevalence among the noninstitutionalized population. Chronic sinusitis and arthritis, the most prevalent chronic conditions, are not killers, although arthritis is often disabling. Hypertension, a risk factor for cerebrovascular and heart diseases, ranks third. Orthopedic and hearing impairments, which

---

TABLE 2–3

CHANGE IN DEATH RATES, SELECTED CAUSES OF DEATH,
UNITED STATES, 1950–1984

(percent)

Cause of Death	1950–1984	1950–1970	1970–1984
Diseases of the heart	− 40.3	− 17.6	− 27.6
Cerebrovascular diseases	− 62.4	− 25.3	− 49.6
Malignant neoplasms	6.5	3.6	2.8
Respiratory system	200.0	121.9	35.2
Breast (female only)	4.5	4.1	0.4
Pneumonia and influenza	− 53.4	− 15.6	− 44.8
Chronic obstructive pulmonary diseases	302.3	200.0	34.1
Chronic liver diseases and cirrhosis	17.6	72.9	− 28.6
Diabetes mellitus	− 35.0	− 1.4	− 32.6
Accidents and adverse effects	39.1	− 6.6	− 34.8
Motor vehicle accidents	− 18.0	17.6	− 30.3
Suicide	5.5	7.3	− 1.7
Homicide and legal intervention	55.6	68.5	− 7.7

NOTE: Based on age-adjusted death rates.
SOURCE: U.S. National Center for Health Statistics, *Health, United States, 1986*, table 21.

TABLE 2-4
CHRONIC CONDITIONS WITH HIGHEST PREVALENCE IN NONINSTITUTIONALIZED POPULATION, 1985, AND LEADING CAUSES OF DEATH, 1984

| *Chronic Conditions with Highest Prevalence, 1985* | | | | *Leading Causes of Death, 1984* | | | |
Condition	Rank	Number of conditions (thousands)	Rate per 1,000 persons	Cause of death	Rank	Number of deaths	Rate per 100,000 persons[a]
Chronic sinusitis	1	32,492	139.0	Diseases of the heart	1	765,114	323.5
Arthritis	2	30,060	128.6	Malignant neoplasms	2	453,492	191.8
Hypertension	3	29,249	125.1	Cerebrovascular diseases	3	154,327	65.3
Deformity or orthopedic impairment	4	26,314	112.6	Accidents and adverse effects	4	92,911	39.3
Hearing impairment	5	21,198	90.7	Chronic obstructive pulmonary diseases and allied conditions	5	69,100	29.2
Hay fever	6	19,642	84.0	Pneumonia and influenza	6	58,894	24.9
Heart disease	7	19,295	82.6	Diabetes mellitus	7	35,787	15.1
Chronic bronchitis	8	11,618	49.7	Suicide	8	29,286	12.4
Hemorrhoids	9	10,359	44.3	Chronic liver diseases and cirrhosis	9	27,317	11.6
Visual impairments	10	8,496	36.4	Atherosclerosis	10	24,462	10.3

a. Crude death rate.
SOURCES: National Center for Health Statistics, *Vital and Health Statistics*, Series 10, no. 160; and *Monthly Vital Statistics Report*, vol. 35, no. 6, supplement 2.

TABLE 2–5

POPULATION OF THE UNITED STATES,
ALL AGES AND SIXTY-FIVE YEARS AND OVER, 1900–2050
(thousands)

		65 Years Old and Over			
	All Ages	Total	65–74	75–84	85 and over
1900	76,303	3,084	2,189	772	123
1910	91,972	3,950	2,793	989	167
1920	105,711	4,933	3,464	1,259	210
1930	122,775	6,634	4,721	1,641	272
1940	131,669	9,019	6,375	2,278	365
1950	150,697	12,270	8,415	3,278	577
1960	179,979	16,675	11,053	4,681	940
1970	204,879	20,085	12,486	6,166	1,432
1980	227,704	25,714	15,652	7,791	2,271
1990	249,657	31,697	18,035	10,349	3,313
2000	267,955	34,921	17,677	12,318	4,926
2010	283,238	39,196	20,318	12,326	6,551
2020	296,597	51,422	29,855	14,486	7,081
2030	304,807	64,580	34,535	21,434	8,611
2040	308,559	66,988	29,272	24,882	12,834
2050	309,488	67,412	30,114	21,263	16,034

NOTE: 1990–2050 are middle series projections.
SOURCES: U.S. Bureau of the Census, *Current Population Reports*, Series P-23, no. 128, and P-25, no. 952.

rank fourth and fifth, are also not killers, though often disabling. It is clear that there is little relationship between the most prevalent chronic conditions and the leading causes of death.

Changing Demographic Structure of the Population

Largely because of declining mortality, the distribution of the population has shifted toward older age groups (table 2–5). The population aged sixty-five and over has grown, will continue to grow for the rest of the twentieth century at a more rapid rate, and is expected to increase well into the next century. In the fifty-year period 1930–1980, the elderly population grew four times as fast as the population under age sixty-five, or 288 percent compared with 74 percent. The U.S. Bureau of the Census projects that both age groups will grow more slowly during the next fifty years but the elderly population will increase at nearly eight times the rate for the population under age sixty-five—151 percent compared with 19 percent.

At the turn of the century only 3.1 million people, or 4.0 percent of the population, were sixty-five and over. Forty years later their numbers had tripled to 9 million, and they made up 6.8 percent of the population. By 1980 they had almost tripled again, to 25.7 million, or 11.3 percent of the population. By the year 2030 it is likely that one out of five Americans will be sixty-five or older, and their total number is projected at 64.6 million—more than twice the total in 1980.

Among those sixty-five years and over, the number and proportion of the very old have also increased rapidly. In 1900 fewer than 125,000 persons were eighty-five or over, and they constituted only 4 percent of the elderly. By 1980 almost 2.3 million persons, or 9 percent of the elderly, were in this age group. And by 2030 the very old population is expected almost to quadruple and to constitute 13 percent of the elderly. Those aged eighty-five and over are expected to be the fastest growing segment of the population, and they are at significantly higher risk of functional dependency, disability, chronic illness, and institutionalization.

These estimates are the middle series projections of the Bureau of the Census.[11] They assume continued improvements in life expectancy and reductions in mortality rates for many of the chronic diseases to the year 2005, based on continuation of past trends, and a leveling off thereafter. Even under more conservative assumptions (the lowest series projections of the Census Bureau), the number of elderly will increase rapidly during the next century—and the number aged eighty-five and over will almost triple from 1980 to 2030.

Longer life may or may not mean improved health. In the rest of this paper, we address the question whether, during the recent period of declining mortality, the health of the population, both elderly and nonelderly, has improved, deteriorated, or remained constant. We focus on disability because it reflects the effects of chronic conditions on major life activities and is associated with a higher demand for medical services and with social and economic disadvantage. We next discuss the size and characteristics of the disabled population, the findings of other studies that have examined trends in chronic conditions and disability, and the problems those studies raise. We hope to provide additional insight by looking at trends in disability resulting from multiple chronic conditions.

Estimating the Size of the Disabled Population

Because definitions of disability vary, the total number of disabled persons is difficult to estimate. The National Health Interview Survey

24

classifies noninstitutionalized persons who report that chronic conditions limit them in the major activity usually associated with their age group.

> The major activities for the age groups are (1) ordinary play for children under 5 years of age, (2) attending school for those 5–17 years of age, (3) working or keeping house for persons 18–69 years of age, and (4) capacity for independent-living (e.g. the ability to bathe, shop, dress, eat and so forth, without the help of another person) for those 70 years of age and over.[12]

Persons are classified into four categories according to the extent to which their activities are limited by chronic conditions: (1) not limited in any way; (2) not limited in the major activity but limited in the kind or amount of other activities; (3) able to perform the major activity but limited in the kind or amount of activity; and (4) unable to perform the major activity.

Table 2–6 compares statistics on the prevalence of disability in 1985 by age from various sources: the 1985 National Health Interview Survey (NHIS), two other recent surveys, and the number of persons receiving benefits from two major public programs. In 1985 about 32.7 million people in the United States, or 14 percent of the total non-institutional population, reported some limitation of their activities as a result of chronic disease or impairment; 4.5 percent were limited but not in their major activity, 5.7 percent were limited in the amount or kind of their major activity, and 3.9 percent—the most severely disabled—were unable to carry on their major activity.

Louis Harris and Associates conducted a survey of disabled Americans aged sixteen and over for the International Center for the Disabled (ICD) in December 1985.[13] The survey slightly modified the NHIS definition of persons with chronic conditions causing limitations of activity to include persons who (1) had disabilities or health problems that prevented full participation in work, school, or other activities; (2) had physical disabilities, seeing, hearing, or speaking impairments, or emotional, mental, or learning disabilities; or (3) considered themselves or were considered by others disabled.

The number of disabled Americans aged sixteen and over was estimated at 27 million, or 14.8 percent of that population group. The numbers of disabled persons in the age groups sixteen to forty-four and forty-five to sixty-four are close to the numbers with activity limitations due to chronic conditions reported in the NHIS. For those sixty-five years and over, the NHIS numbers are one-third higher. This difference may be due partly to differences in definitions of disability for the elderly population.

The ICD survey revealed that the disabled have less education

25

TABLE 2-6

COMPARISON OF STATISTICS ON THE PREVALENCE OF DISABILITY BY AGE, 1985

Age Group	National Health Interview Survey				ICD Survey of Disabled Americans	Long-Term Care Survey, 1982	Social Security Disability Insurance Beneficiaries	SSI Disability Beneficiaries
	With activity limitation	Limited, but not in major activity	Limited in amount or kind of major activity	Unable to carry on major activity				
	Number (thousands)							
Total	32,726	10,455	13,228	9,044	27,000[a]		2,657[b]	2,551
Under 18	3,221	910	2,020	292	—		—	257
18–44	8,391	2,737	3,592	2,062	8,802[c]		2,657[b]	896
45–64	10,405	2,619	3,897	3,889	10,179	—	—	893
65 and over	10,709	4,189	3,719	2,802	7,992	5,074	—	505
65–69	3,641	748	1,318	1,576	—	1,109	—	243
70 and over	7,068	3,441	2,401	1,226	—	3,965	—	262

Percentage of Population Group

Total	14.0	4.5	5.7	3.9	14.8[a]	—	1.8[b]	1.1
Under 18	5.1	1.5	3.2	0.5	—	—	—	0.4
18–44	8.4	2.8	3.6	2.1	8.2[c]	—	1.8[b]	0.9
45–64	23.4	5.9	8.8	8.7	22.7	—	—	2.0
65 and over	39.6	15.5	13.8	10.4	28.0	19.1	—	1.9
65–69	39.2	8.1	14.2	17.0	—	12.8	—	2.6
70 and over	39.8	19.4	13.5	6.9	—	22.2	—	1.5

a. Persons aged sixteen and over.
b. Disabled workers aged eighteen to sixty-four.
c. Persons aged sixteen to forty-four.
SOURCES: National Center for Health Statistics, *Vital and Health Statistics*, Series 10, no. 160, tables 67 and 68, 1986; International Center for the Disabled, Survey of Disabled Americans, 1986; *Health Care Financing Review* (Summer 1986), pp. 33–49; *Social Security Bulletin* (June 1986), p. 70; and *Social Security Bulletin* (June 1986), p. 87.

and are much poorer than those who are not disabled. It also found significant barriers to work: two-thirds of all disabled persons between the ages of sixteen and sixty-four are not employed although two-thirds of those not working say they want to work. The majority of those not working and not in the labor force depend on insurance payments or government benefits for support, and the majority of those who receive benefits say that they are the main wage earners in their households.

The 1982 Long-Term Care Survey conducted by the Health Care Financing Administration identified approximately 5 million functionally impaired elderly persons living in the community, or 19.1 percent of the total elderly outside institutions.[14] Here the definition was based entirely on ability to perform daily activities. The number of those aged seventy and over found to be functionally impaired was 9 percent higher than the number classified as limited in their major activity by the NHIS.

The two major federal disability programs in the United States are SSDI for the disabled working-age population and SSI for disabled children, working-age adults, and elderly persons who are poor. In December 1985 some 2.7 million disabled workers aged eighteen to sixty-four and more than 600,000 others who were disabled in childhood or are disabled widows or widowers received benefits under the SSDI program, and 1.8 million disabled adults received benefits under the SSI program. We estimate that about 4.4 million disabled persons of working age (eighteen to sixty-four years) received benefits under the SSDI or SSI programs, as shown below:

Type of Beneficiary	Number (thousands)
SSDI	
Disabled workers	2,657
Adults disabled in childhood	516
Disabled widows and widowers	106
SSI	
Disabled adults	1,789
Dual entitlement	−685
Total	4,383

From a policy perspective, it would be important to know what proportion those 4.4 million persons are of the total population of severely disabled people aged eighteen to sixty-four. This figure is not readily available but can be estimated in several ways.

One rough estimate may be derived from the 1978 Survey of Disability and Work conducted by the Social Security Administration.

The total number of severely disabled persons—those who reported being "unable to work altogether or unable to work regularly"—was estimated at 10.9 million. Of this total 27 percent received SSDI or SSI benefits in 1978.[15]

Another estimate may be derived from the 1985 ICD survey of disabled Americans, which found that three-fifths of the working-age disabled population not in the labor force received some public or private insurance benefits. Of all the disabled who received benefits, 63 percent received SSDI or SSI payments. A small fraction of the disabled receive benefits while they still work a limited number of hours (earning less than $300 a month). If we assume that most persons who report receiving SSDI or SSI payments are out of the labor force, the ICD survey suggests that up to half the severely disabled received disability payments under these two programs.

Yet a third estimate can be obtained from the number of persons who report in the NHIS being unable to work because of a chronic condition. The number identified in table 2–6 as being unable to perform their major activity cannot be used as a denominator, because some persons not limited in their major activity may still be unable to work. We have estimated from the 1984 NHIS that 7.7 million persons aged eighteen to sixty-four reported being unable to work at all. We thus estimate that up to 57 percent of severely disabled persons of working age received cash benefits under the two major public programs for the disabled.

The three estimates range from 27 to 57 percent, depending on whether persons who work irregularly are included in the definition of the severely disabled. We conclude that at least 3.3 million persons in the United States who are unable to work because of health problems receive no benefits under SSDI or SSI. Many may be impaired severely enough to qualify for disability benefits under social security. The ICD survey indicates that many in this group are economically vulnerable. More research is needed on the characteristics of this group of disabled nonbeneficiaries.

The highest estimate of the disabled population, 33 million people, is provided by the NHIS. Not surprisingly, persons who are limited in activity by chronic conditions are more restricted in their daily activities and are high users of medical resources. In 1979 persons with limitations of their activities due to chronic conditions averaged 9.5 visits to physicians in contrast with 3.9 visits for persons with no such limitations. They also had 38.3 hospitalizations per 100 persons, compared with 9.8 for those with no limitations. The 14.6 percent of people who were limited in activity because of a chronic condition accounted for 29 percent of contacts with physicians, 40 percent of hospitalizations, 58 percent of hospital days of care, and 47 percent of all the days people spent in bed for reasons of health.[16]

Many persons who are limited in their major activities need the help of another person or a device in performing the basic activities of daily living. Such persons are highly likely to need long-term care and may be at risk for institutionalization. The 1979–1980 home care supplement of the NHIS provides estimates of the proportion of persons with various limitations in major activity who need the help of another person or a device in performing basic activities.[17]

During the period 1979–1980, 6.4 million persons, or 3 percent of the total noninstitutionalized population, required such functional assistance (table 2–7). Of all those needing such assistance, 820,000 persons, or 12.8 percent, reported no limitations in their usual activity. The other 5.6 million who needed help with daily living constituted 17.7 percent of the 31.5 million persons reporting some limitation in activity. About 47 percent of the population who need functional assistance are not elderly, and more than half of these are forty-five to sixty-four. Thus significant disability occurs early in the life span, causing severe disruptions in economic and family life.

The proportion of the population with activity limitations requiring functional assistance increased with the severity of the limitation, rising from 5.3 percent of those limited in other than their major activity to 14.4 percent of those limited in the amount or kind of major activity and 36.5 percent of those unable to perform their major activity. It is clear that not all persons limited in activity because of chronic conditions need help to function, but a much higher proportion of the more severely disabled persons do require such assistance. Furthermore, more than half of all persons who do require functional assistance are able to perform their major activity to some degree. Thus many persons who require functional assistance manage to avoid disability in other major life activities.

Trends in Chronic Conditions and Disability

There is considerable disagreement over past and future trends in chronic conditions and disability. James F. Fries predicts that improvements in life style will delay the onset of disability and compress morbidity into the older ages. He foresees a continuing decline in premature death and the emergence of a pattern of natural death at the end of the biological life span.[18] Morton Kramer argues that the prevalence of chronic disease and disability will increase as life expectancy increases, leading to a "pandemic" of mental disorders and chronic diseases.[19] Ernest M. Gruenberg sees the increasing prevalence of chronic conditions due to improvements in medical technology as "the failures of success."[20] Edward L. Schneider and Jacob A. Brody conclude that very old people are increasing rapidly and predict that the average period of diminished vigor will lengthen, chronic diseases will occupy a larger proportion of our life span, and the needs for medical care in later life will increase substantially.[21]

TABLE 2–7

PERSONS NEEDING FUNCTIONAL ASSISTANCE, BY LIMITATION STATUS,
1979–1980

| | | Limitation Status | | | |
Sex and Age	Total Needing Functional Assistance	Not limited	Limited but not in major activity	Limited in amount or kind of major activity	Unable to carry on major activity
		Number (thousands)			
Total	6,399	820	416	2,255	2,908
Males	2,452	312	130	402	1,608
Females	3,947	508	286	1,852	1,301
Age					
Under 17	352	197	35	109	12
17–44	996	183	96	376	341
45–64	1,662	144	91	601	826
65–74	1,337	124	69	506	639
75–84	1,362	107	76	468	711
85 and over	689	65	49	195	380
		Percentage of Total Population in Category			
Total	3.0	0.4	5.3	14.4	36.5
Male	2.3	0.3	3.5	6.9	27.3
Female	3.5	0.5	7.0	18.8	62.9
Age					
Under 17	0.6	0.3	3.3	9.8	12.6
17–44	1.1	0.2	3.3	9.4	32.7
45–64	3.8	0.4	4.0	11.3	29.5
65–74			7.5	6.0	29.9
75–84	14.3[a]	2.3[a]	15.6	28.7	51.5
85 and over			40.7	48.0	73.7

NOTE: Includes persons who need assistance because of a chronic health problem in basic physical or home management activities, who usually stay in bed all or most of the time, or who experience bowel or urinary trouble.

a. Percentage of population aged sixty-five and over.

SOURCE: Computed from the 1979–1980 Home Care Supplement of the National Health Interview Survey micro data tapes.

31

Kenneth G. Manton views human aging and mortality as dynamic multidimensional processes in which chronic degenerative diseases play an essential role. His concept of "dynamic equilibrium" implies that the severity and rate of progression of chronic disease are directly related to mortality changes, so that with reduced mortality comes a corresponding reduction in the rate of aging of the vital bodily organ system. He believes that the severity of chronic diseases will be reduced or the rate of progression slowed with a consequent reduction in mortality rates and an increase in life expectancy.[22]

Future changes in the incidence and prevalence of chronic illness and disability among the growing number of elderly persons will obviously play an important role in the demand for medical services. Rice and Jacob J. Feldman estimated the effect of the aging of the population on health status, the use of health services, and health expenditures by applying 1980 rates for specific age groups for each sex to the projected populations for the years 2000, 2020, and 2040.[23] As the elderly population more than doubles from 1980 to 2040, they found, the number of elderly persons with limitations of activities of daily living will more than triple, hospital days will also triple, and the number of nursing home residents will almost quadruple.

Lois M. Verbrugge analyzed past trends in specific chronic conditions, disability, and mortality for middle-aged and older persons reported in the NHIS over a twenty-three-year period, 1958 to 1981. She examined both "killers"—chronic conditions that often lead to death—and "nonkillers" that seldom cause death.[24] For middle-aged people ten of the eleven chronic diseases studied had become more prevalent, with cancer, diabetes, heart disease, and hypertension showing especially large increases; over the same period, though, mortality rates declined for eight of those diseases. The relationship between morbidity and mortality trends for older people was similar to that for middle-aged people.

Of conditions that do not kill, musculoskeletal problems increased dramatically both in prevalence and as a cause of limitations of activity. Nonfatal respiratory problems, including sinusitis and hay fever, also increased; ulcers and other digestive diseases decreased. Many impairments declined in prevalence among the elderly population, including visual, hearing, lower extremity and hip, and multiple orthopedic impairments, and they were less limiting.

Verbrugge also noted a consistent, gradual increase since the late 1960s in limitations of activity among persons aged forty-five and over, a gradual increase in days of restricted activity per person for the total population, and, to a lesser extent, an increase in bed disability days. Besides possible changes in "true" incidence and survival rates, she suggests, these increases may be caused by a variety of factors: persons may be more willing to cut down their activities to accommodate chronic conditions, perhaps because of earlier diagnosis and increased awareness even without any "true" changes in the prevalence of chronic conditions; they may change their jobs and other activities at earlier stages of impairment than in the past; they may be more likely to adopt the "sick" role than in the past; they may restrict their activities more during flare-ups of chronic conditions; and they may have more social and economic supports available. Thus changing accommodation to social, medical, and economic conditions could have increased both the prevalence of limitations and the number of disability days without changes in actual impairment.

Ronald W. Wilson and Thomas F. Drury also suggest that, because of health promotion recommendations, persons with chronic conditions may be more active and this greater activity may mean that there will be more days in which they cut down on the things they usually do.[25] Wilson and Drury give as an example the elderly person who in the past may have had no inclination to exercise but might now jog around the block. The flare-up of a chronic condition might have had no effect on this person's activity in the past but would now prevent him or her from jogging for one or several days that would probably be reported as restricted activity days.

A major component of the increasing prevalence of limitations in the activity of persons aged eighteen to sixty-four is work disability. Thomas N. Chirikos examined trends in work disability from 1950 to 1982, using data from a variety of population surveys, and concluded that reported work disability had significantly increased.[26] It has been suggested, however, that the increase in the proportion of middle-aged persons unable to work was stimulated by higher disability benefits under the SSDI program. Higher benefits and higher unemployment rates may cause persons with less severe impairments to claim disability.[27]

All these arguments suggest that persons who claim to be disabled will, to some extent, be less impaired than in the past because of changing awareness, financial incentives, or economic conditions. Because the same factors may cause persons to report more disability days, such days are not a sufficient indicator of impairment. An alternative measure of severity is the existence of multiple conditions. It is generally recognized that the coexistence of several chronic diseases has a profoundly negative effect on health and functional independence.[28] Analyzing the 1976 NHIS, which contained an arthritis supplement, Edward H. Yelin, Jane S. Kramer, and Wallace V. Epstein stressed multiple conditions in determining the functional capacity of persons over fifty-five with arthritis.[29]

Since persons have no obvious incentives to report multiple conditions, this indicator should be less influenced by the factors mentioned earlier—although greater awareness could cause more conditions to be reported in the absence of any "true" change. Because the high use of medical care by persons with disabilities implies that they are a highly informed population, we would expect that increasing awareness is not the major factor. Changing accommodation to chronic conditions is less likely to bias reported activity restrictions among persons with multiple conditions, since they are highly impaired. Rather, trends in the prevalence of persons with multiple chronic conditions and their "illness behavior" indicate changes in the true health status of this population more clearly than traditional indicators do. We believe, therefore, that the trend in the number of conditions reported to cause disability is an additional indicator of whether the health status of disabled persons is changing.

Trends in Multiple Chronic Conditions

To reach a better understanding of past morbidity trends, changes in the severity of disabling conditions, and their policy implications, we now examine trends in the prevalence of multiple chronic disabling conditions and the burden associated with them over the period 1969–1971 to 1979–1981. This period saw significant declines in death rates for many of the chronic diseases. We might expect a concomitant decline in the prevalence of chronic conditions and in the severity of chronic illnesses.

The data from the NHIS are a major resource for analysis of the effect of multiple chronic conditions on functional disability and on the use of medical care. To provide statistically reliable estimates, we combined the data from the NHIS public use tapes for two three-year periods, 1969–1971 and 1979–1981.

Prevalence and Number of Limiting Chronic Conditions. During the period 1969–1971 to 1979–1981 the prevalence of limitations in activity due to chronic conditions increased 22 percent, from 119 to 145 per 1,000 persons (table 2–8). The increase was greater for women than for men, and there were substantial differences among age groups. The largest increase, 40 percent, occurred among those under seventeen. This larger increase has also been documented by Paul W. Newacheck and his colleagues.[30] They attribute the increase in limitations in activity among children to shifting perceptions of illness by parents, educators, and physicians, reflecting the "new morbidity" of childhood illnesses with a greater psychosocial component.

34

The next largest increase in the prevalence of limitations in activity due to chronic conditions, 21 percent, was in the age group forty-five to sixty-four years, generally considered the period of most productive employment. Several studies have also documented a rise in work disability attributed to a variety of factors, including the reduction in age-adjusted mortality with its concomitant increasing risk of being disabled by chronic conditions, socioeconomic factors such as the availability of more generous social insurance programs, and greater awareness of diseases because of earlier diagnosis.[31]

The trends for the noninstitutionalized elderly varied. An increase in the prevalence of limitations of 14 percent for those aged

TABLE 2–8

PREVALENCE OF LIMITATION OF ACTIVITY DUE TO
CHRONIC CONDITIONS AND NUMBER OF CONDITIONS PER PERSON,
BY SEX AND AGE, 1969–1971 AND 1979–1981

Sex and Age	1969–1971	1979–1981	Percent Change
	Prevalence (rate per 1,000 persons)		
Total	118.66	144.55	21.8
Males	124.43	146.70	17.9
Females	113.30	142.54	25.8
Age			
Under 17	27.54	38.47	39.7
17–44	76.77	86.03	12.1
45–64	197.75	239.66	21.2
65–74	363.14	412.57	13.6
75–84	508.33	506.80	−0.3
85 and over	667.34	648.63	−2.8
	Limiting Conditions per Person		
Total	1.318	1.483	12.5
Males	1.306	1.446	10.7
Females	1.331	1.519	14.1
Age			
Under 17	1.135	1.197	5.5
17–44	1.172	1.268	8.2
45–64	1.352	1.557	15.2
65–74	1.420	1.618	13.9
75–84	1.449	1.655	14.2
85 and over	1.378	1.608	16.7

SOURCE: Computed from the National Health Interview Survey micro data tapes.

sixty-five to seventy-four contrasted with a decline of less than 1 percent for persons seventy-five to eighty-four and a 3 percent decline for those eighty-five and over. This would seem to indicate that the health of the oldest old living in the community has not worsened. This could be due, however, to differential rates of selection of the oldest old disabled into institutions.

The number of chronic conditions causing limitation of activity increased 12.5 percent, from 1.32 to 1.48 per person, over this period (table 2–8 and figure 2–2). This increase occurred for all ages, with the greatest increase (16.7 percent) for those aged eighty-five and over. Thus, while the proportion of the oldest old who are disabled decreased, the number of conditions reported increased, suggesting worsening health for persons in this age group.

The number of limiting conditions per person increased with age in both periods up to age eighty-five. For the oldest old the number dropped slightly. This may be due to changing rates of selection of the disabled into institutions at the oldest ages. Comparisons over time of the health of the oldest old living in the community thus need to control for changes in the selection of older persons into institutions, which we cannot address here.

The prevalence of limitation of activity due to chronic conditions and the number of limiting conditions per person are shown in table 2–9 and figures 2–3 and 2–4 by limitation status. The percentage increases between 1969–1971 and 1979–1981 in prevalence per 1,000 persons range from 16 percent for those limited in the amount and kind of their major activity to 29 percent for those unable to carry on their major activity. The largest percentage increase for men was for the more severely disabled; for women it was among those who were limited but not in their major activity.

The prevalence of activity limitation due to chronic conditions increases sharply with age in both periods, regardless of limitation status, but the relative changes vary with age. For young people under seventeen by far the largest increase between the two periods was for those reporting limitations in the amount and kind of major activity. For the adult population the largest increase, 48 percent, was for those in their middle years (ages forty-five to sixty-four) who report being unable to carry on their major activity. For those in their later years (ages seventy-five and over), the prevalence of activity-limiting chronic conditions declined slightly for the most disabled persons.

The number of limiting chronic conditions per person increased 5.5 percent for those least limited but 9 to 10 percent for those more limited. This pattern held for all age groups. Among those eighty-five

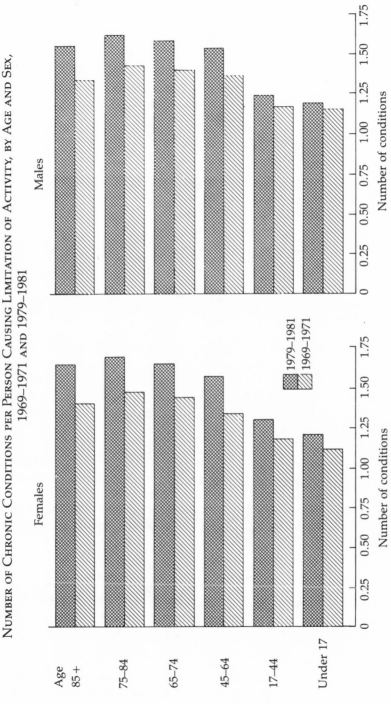

FIGURE 2-2

NUMBER OF CHRONIC CONDITIONS PER PERSON CAUSING LIMITATION OF ACTIVITY, BY AGE AND SEX, 1969–1971 AND 1979–1981

TABLE 2–9

Prevalence of Limitation of Activity Due to Chronic Conditions and Number of Conditions per Person, by Sex, Age, and Limitation Status, 1969–1971 and 1979–1981

Sex and Age	1969–1971			1979–1981			Percent Change, 1969–1971 to 1979–1981		
	Limited but not in major activity	Limited in amount and kind of major activity	Unable to carry on major activity	Limited but not in major activity	Limited in amount and kind of major activity	Unable to carry on major activity	Limited but not in major activity	Limited in amount and kind of major activity	Unable to carry on major activity
	Prevalence (rate per 1,000 persons)								
Total	27.87	62.02	28.77	35.54	71.78	37.23	27.5	15.7	29.4
Males	29.09	52.08	43.25	34.62	54.72	57.37	19.0	5.1	32.6
Females	26.74	71.26	15.30	36.41	87.69	18.45	36.2	23.1	20.6
Age									
Under 17	14.29	11.51	1.74	18.10	18.78	1.61	26.7	63.2	–7.5
17–44	27.09	40.60	9.08	31.37	43.14	11.52	15.8	6.3	26.9
45–64	40.24	113.13	44.39	51.36	122.77	65.54	27.6	8.5	47.6
65–74	45.20	191.09	126.86	61.66	207.52	143.40	36.4	8.6	13.0
75–84	62.23	239.80	206.37	70.47	237.99	198.34	13.2	–0.8	–3.9
85 and over	64.23	258.14	345.41	77.36	243.89	327.46	20.4	–5.5	–5.2

Limiting Conditions per Person

Total	1.162	1.295	1.507	1.226	1.425	1.645	5.5	10.0	9.2
Males	1.125	1.221	1.504	1.182	1.304	1.628	5.1	6.8	8.2
Females	1.200	1.346	1.516	1.265	1.496	1.694	5.4	11.1	11.7
Age									
Under 17	1.114	1.144	1.157	1.154	1.211	1.260	3.6	5.9	8.9
17–44	1.096	1.188	1.289	1.157	1.281	1.402	5.6	7.8	8.8
45–64	1.200	1.322	1.567	1.269	1.482	1.698	5.8	12.1	8.4
65–74	1.276	1.378	1.538	1.328	1.525	1.689	4.1	10.7	9.8
75–84	1.299	1.383	1.545	1.378	1.531	1.697	6.1	10.7	9.8
85 and over	1.187	1.275	1.467	1.310	1.469	1.600	10.4	15.2	9.1

SOURCE: Computed from the National Health Interview Survey micro data tapes.

FIGURE 2–3

PREVALENCE OF LIMITATION OF ACTIVITY DUE TO CHRONIC CONDITIONS,
BY AGE AND LIMITATION STATUS, 1969–1971 AND 1979–1981
(per 1,000 persons)

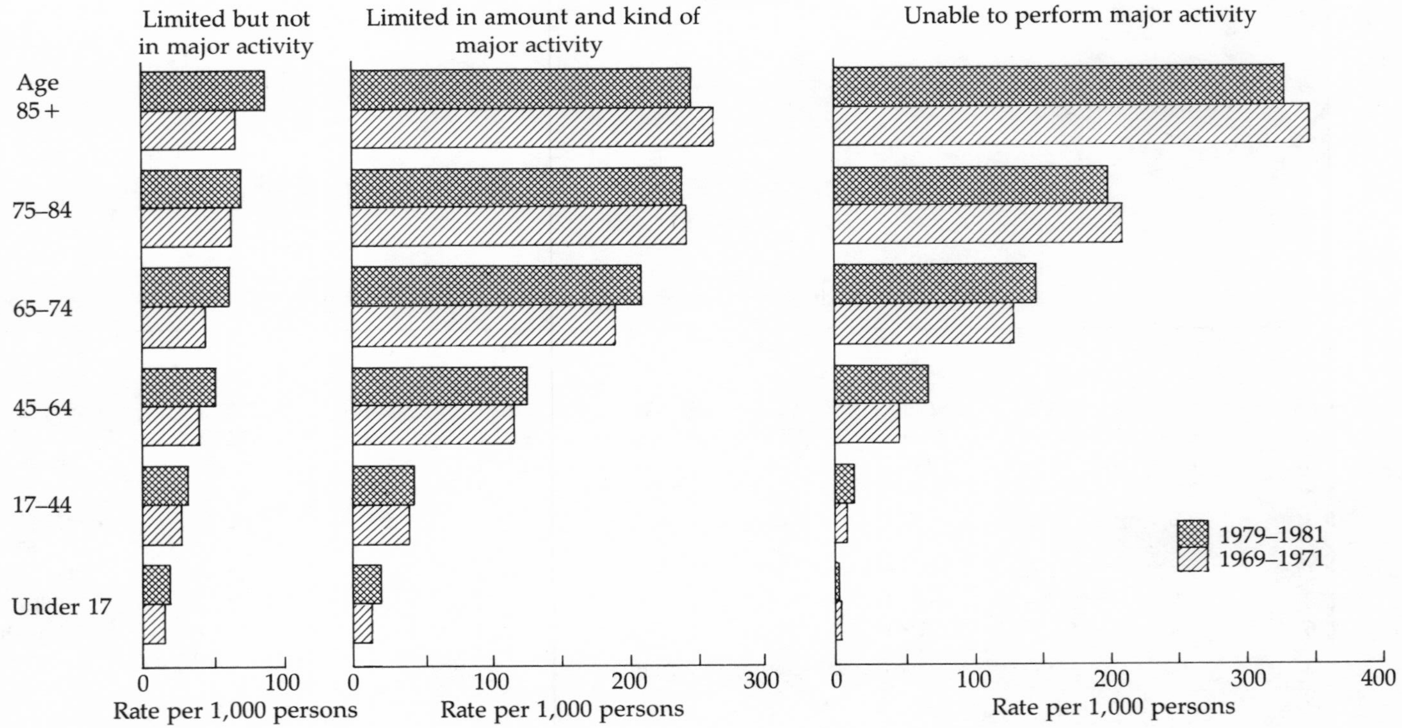

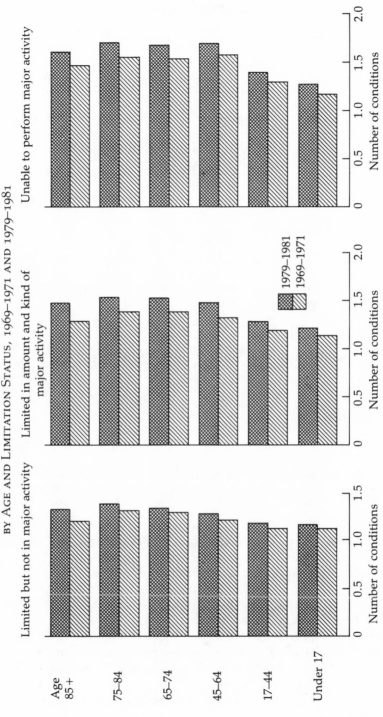

FIGURE 2-4

Number of Chronic Conditions per Person Causing Limitation of Activity,
by Age and Limitation Status, 1969–1971 and 1979–1981

TABLE 2–10

RESTRICTED ACTIVITY AND BED DISABILITY DAYS PER PERSON
LIMITED IN ACTIVITY, BY SEX AND AGE, 1969–1971 AND 1979–1981

Sex and Age	1969–1971	1979–1981	Percent Change
	Restricted Activity Days per Person		
Total	55.8	68.7	23.1
Males	50.0	61.2	22.4
Females	61.8	75.8	22.7
Age			
Under 17	34.2	37.3	9.1
17–44	46.8	60.2	28.6
45–64	62.2	77.6	24.8
65–74	61.3	72.3	17.9
75–84	60.4	75.1	24.3
85 and over	56.5	67.8	20.0
	Bed Disability Days per Person		
Total	21.3	22.3	4.7
Males	18.0	18.4	2.2
Females	24.6	26.0	5.7
Age			
Under 17	15.0	13.8	− 8.0
17–44	15.9	18.9	18.9
45–64	22.2	24.0	8.1
65–74	24.0	22.8	− 5.0
75–84	24.9	25.9	4.0
85 and over	34.8	33.0	− 5.2

SOURCE: Computed from the National Health Interview Survey micro data tapes.

and over a 15 percent increase was reported for those limited in the amount and kind of their major activity and a 9 percent increase for those unable to perform their major activity.

Restricted Activity and Bed Disability Days. Days of restricted activity per person limited in activity rose 23 percent over the period, from fifty-six to sixty-nine days (table 2–10 and figure 2–5). Increases occurred for all age groups and for men and women. Although a similar trend has been noted for the entire U.S. population, fully 72 percent of the total increase in days of restricted activity occurred among the population with limitations in activity because of chronic conditions.[32]

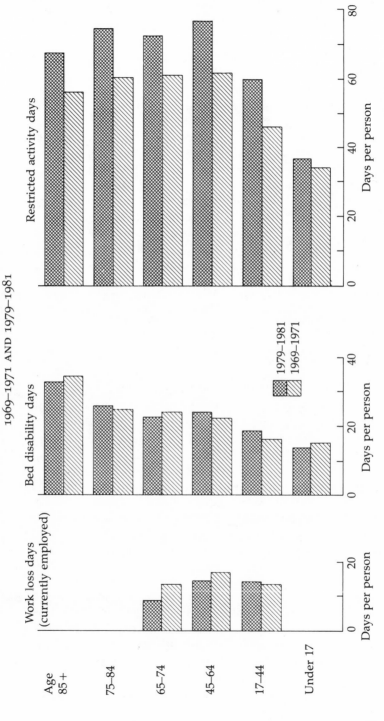

FIGURE 2–5
DISABILITY DAYS PER PERSON LIMITED IN ACTIVITY, BY AGE,
1969–1971 AND 1979–1981

Work loss days
(currently employed)

Bed disability days

Restricted activity days

1979–1981
1969–1971

Days per person

Days per person

Days per person

Age
85+

75–84

65–74

45–64

17–44

Under 17

Bed disability days remained relatively constant, at about twenty-one or twenty-two days, while days of lost work for the currently employed limited population declined for persons ages forty-five years and older, possibly indicating some selection in the workplace toward healthier persons (figure 2–5). For both periods, however, the numbers of restricted activity and bed disability days increased substantially with the number of conditions reported, as shown in table 2–11. Persons with two conditions had about 50 percent more restricted activity and bed disability days than those with one condition; persons with three or more conditions had about twice as many such days as those with only one. Days of restricted activity increased fairly substantially among the population aged seventeen to sixty-four with two or more conditions but declined among persons eighty-five and over with multiple conditions.

Severity of limitation and the number of conditions reported apparently interact to affect the number of days of restricted activity. People with three or more conditions who were unable to perform their major activity showed the largest absolute increase in restricted activity days, approximately 21 more days per person per year (figure 2–6).

Medical Care Utilization. Two measures of the use of medical care are visits to physicians and hospital days, shown in table 2–12. During the period 1969–1971 to 1979–1981, the total number of visits to physicians for persons limited in activity by chronic conditions (excluding visits by physicians to hospital inpatients) increased 33 percent, but the number per person remained stable. The percentage changes per person varied with age: a 3.2 percent increase for those under age forty-four, no change for those forty-five to sixty-four, and declines ranging from 1 to 7 percent for subgroups of the elderly. The number of visits in both periods was about nine or ten per person per year for all age groups except those eighty-five and over; this oldest group had less than seven visits per person.

Hospital days reflect the number of persons hospitalized and the average length of stay. During the period 1970 to 1980 the total number of patients discharged from short-stay hospitals rose 30 percent while the average length of stay declined from 7.8 to 7.3 days.[33] The total days of care for all persons increased 21 percent. The data on hospital days for persons limited in activity by chronic conditions were similar to data for the total population. Total days of care increased 15 percent but days per capita declined 14 percent from 1969–1971 to 1979–1981. Hospital days per person decreased more for men than for women; the largest decline (23 percent) was for those under age seventeen and the smallest (7 percent) for the oldest population. Thus, although numbers of physicians' visits per person remained relatively stable and hospital days per person declined, the growth in the population limited in activity by chronic illness placed a greater burden on the services of physicians and, possibly, hospitals because of the greater need of the disabled for medical services.

We have considered whether the greater frequency with which disabling conditions are reported can be attributed to changes in survey coding procedures. Certain conditions, such as hypertension and heart disease, were combined less frequently under the International Classification of Diseases adapted for use in the United States (ICDA-9) than under the previous version. The NHIS changed to ICDA-9 in 1979. The proportions reporting multiple conditions and the mean number of conditions in 1977, 1978, and 1979 show that the increase was gradual and was not due to the changes in coding.

Part of the increase in reporting of multiple disabling conditions may be due to greater awareness, since access to medical services increased significantly over this period.[34] Studies have shown that chronic conditions are both highly underreported and overreported in interview surveys, compared with medical records.[35] Convergence is higher, however, for conditions that affect the individual significantly. In a study conducted in the late 1950s, 70 percent of all conditions diagnosed by medical providers were reported by persons with limitations of their activity, but only 45 percent by persons without such limitations.[36]

Improvements in reporting could account for the trend toward more conditions being mentioned as causing disability. A recent study based on provider checks built into the National Medical Care Expenditure Survey (NMCES), however, suggests that there probably has been no improvement in reporting.[37] In this study 70 percent of conditions diagnosed by providers were not reported in interviews while 60 percent of conditions reported in interviews were not diagnosed by providers. In the studies mentioned earlier, 50 percent of conditions were underreported while 40 percent were overreported.

Differences in study design may account for part of the higher degrees of underreporting and overreporting found in the NMCES. More thought and research has to be given to the comparisons of self-reported conditions with medical assessments, and priority should be given to the conduct of such studies so that we can better understand temporal patterns in health status. No evidence seems to show that reporting has improved.

Increases in the number of chronic disabling conditions reported in recent years may be due to improved survival of disabled persons.

45

TABLE 2-11

Restricted Activity and Bed Disability Days per Person Limited in Activity, by Sex, Age, and Number of Conditions, 1969–1971 and 1979–1981

	1969–1971			1979–1981			Percent Change, 1969–1971 to 1979–1981		
	One condition	Two conditions	Three conditions	One condition	Two conditions	Three conditions	One condition	Two conditions	Three conditions
	Restricted Activity Days per Person								
Total	48.4	73.6	99.0	56.8	83.5	113.6	17.4	13.5	14.7
Males	43.4	66.8	90.0	50.8	75.7	105.5	17.1	13.3	17.2
Females	53.6	79.7	108.0	62.9	90.4	120.1	17.4	13.4	11.2
Age									
Under 17	33.5	34.5	71.2	35.3	45.4	61.3	5.4	31.6	–13.9
17–44	42.9	66.3	94.2	54.4	73.0	114.2	26.8	10.1	21.2
45–64	54.7	76.8	103.2	62.4	92.9	124.4	14.1	21.0	20.5
65–74	52.6	73.1	102.5	58.4	84.7	107.4	11.0	15.9	4.8
75–84	49.7	81.1	90.1	61.7	84.8	109.0	24.1	4.6	21.0
85 and over	43.7	86.7	109.1	59.4	71.8	97.2	35.9	–17.2	–10.9

Bed Disability Days per Person

Total	18.4	28.0	38.5	18.3	26.7	38.1	−0.5	−4.6	−1.0
Males	15.6	23.5	34.5	15.2	21.9	33.5	−2.6	−6.8	−2.9
Females	21.3	32.0	42.6	21.5	31.0	41.7	0.9	−3.1	−2.1
Age									
Under 17	14.8	14.9	23.4	13.1	16.3	23.0	−11.5	9.4	−1.7
17–44	14.6	22.8	30.6	16.3	25.4	42.0	11.6	11.4	37.3
45–64	19.4	27.6	38.3	19.6	27.4	39.8	1.0	−0.7	3.9
65–74	21.0	27.5	39.6	19.1	26.0	32.6	−9.0	−5.5	−17.7
75–84	20.8	33.3	35.6	20.2	29.2	41.6	−2.9	−12.3	16.9
85 and over	27.2	49.0	74.9	30.5	36.4	39.1	12.1	−25.7	−47.8

SOURCE: Computed from the National Health Interview Survey micro data tapes.

48

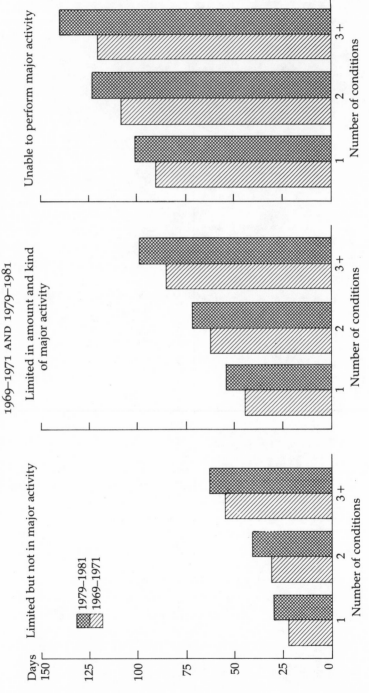

FIGURE 2-6

RESTRICTED ACTIVITY DAYS PER PERSON LIMITED IN ACTIVITY,
BY LIMITATION STATUS AND NUMBER OF CHRONIC CONDITIONS,
1969–1971 AND 1979–1981

This explanation may also account for the increased prevalence rates of disability and the greater restriction of activity experienced by persons with multiple disabling conditions in this period of declining mortality. Since persons are experiencing significantly greater disability according to these several indicators, it is unlikely that greater awareness can account for all these trends. Improved survival of the disabled appears to be a more likely explanation.

Conclusions and Recommendations

As people appear to have become more disabled under conditions of declining mortality, the question whether public and private disability insurance and medical care programs provide adequate coverage is a critical one. At least 3.3 million persons aged eighteen to sixty-four who are unable to work because of health problems receive no benefits under the two largest public disability programs, SSDI and SSI. During the period studied the number of both awards and beneficiaries under SSDI and SSI declined significantly.[38] In 1980, 35 percent of all awards were granted after being initially denied by state offices whose decisions were subsequently reversed by administrative law judges. This administrative tightening in the interpretation of eligibility rules probably deterred many persons from applying for benefits and greatly increased the litigiousness of the application process. Awards under SSDI continued to decline until they reached a low of 621,000 in 1983, down from 1.26 million in 1975. They increased slightly to 714,000 in 1985; nevertheless, during this period of rising disability, a significant tightening in the interpretation of eligibility rules has delayed the application process and led to more litigation.

We also question whether health care is adequately covered for those who do receive disability benefits. As James Lubitz and Penelope Pine have shown, some of the sickest disabled beneficiaries under SSDI do not survive the two-and-one-half-year period they must wait before they are covered under Medicare.[39] The majority of them have no private health insurance. Catastrophic health insurance proposals should include coverage for the working-age disabled.

Fries argues that morbidity will be compressed to a short period at the end of the life span. Past trends indicate that activity-limiting chronic conditions are occurring with greater frequency early in life. Whether disability continues to be more prevalent in middle-aged and older populations as time goes on depends on cohort succession. We may be at a stage where secondary and tertiary prevention efforts, which improve survival but do not necessarily cure chronic conditions, are mainly responsible for increasing disability. If primary

TABLE 2-12

PHYSICIANS' VISITS AND HOSPITAL DAYS, PERSONS LIMITED IN ACTIVITY, BY SEX AND AGE, 1969–1971 AND 1979–1981

Sex and Age	1969–1971		1979–1981		Percent Change	
	Number (thousands)	Per person	Number (thousands)	Per person	Number	Per person
	Physicians' Visits					
Total	229,484	9.68	305,091	9.61	32.9	−0.7
Males	102,244	8.53	132,410	8.52	29.5	−0.1
Females	127,240	10.84	172,681	10.66	35.7	−1.7
Age						
Under 17	18,241	9.93	22,993	10.25	26.1	3.2
17–44	54,102	9.67	80,295	9.98	48.4	3.2
45–64	82,676	10.13	106,110	10.13	28.3	0.0
65–74	41,385	9.61	57,685	9.17	39.4	−4.6
75–84	27,823	9.15	30,980	8.54	11.3	−6.7
85 and over	5,257	6.78	7,027	6.69	33.7	−1.3

Hospital Days

Total	101,916	4.30	116,986	3.69	14.8	−14.2
Males	53,562	4.47	58,237	3.75	8.7	−16.1
Females	48,354	4.12	58,749	3.63	21.5	−11.9
Age						
Under 17	4,761	2.59	4,486	2.00	−5.8	−22.8
17–44	21,605	3.86	25,054	3.11	16.0	−19.4
45–64	34,788	4.26	40,335	3.85	15.9	−9.6
65–74	20,936	4.86	25,302	4.02	20.9	−17.3
75–84	15,811	5.20	16,759	4.62	6.0	−11.2
85 and over	4,014	5.18	5,050	4.80	25.8	−7.3

SOURCE: Computed from the National Health Interview Survey micro data tapes.

prevention efforts succeed in postponing the incidence of disability to older ages, disability rates may decline in younger cohorts, and the trends noted here may be reversed. Otherwise the need and demand for health and social services for a larger chronically ill population will grow. The growing numbers of chronically ill and disabled persons of all ages will mean an increasing need for rehabilitation, income support, and long-term care services to maintain their economic status and independence at home and to avoid placement in institutions.[40]

For the population under seventy-five, the data examined suggest worsening health at all ages. This is consistent with declining mortality rates for all ages. While it seems plausible that persons may be surviving longer with disabling chronic conditions, the data on multiple chronic conditions do not explain the increase in work disability at the older working ages. Other factors, such as the availability of private pensions and private and public disability insurance benefits, probably affect this trend.

For the population seventy-five and over, the trend data are difficult to interpret. Although multiple chronic conditions increased, the prevalence of limitation of activity due to chronic conditions remained fairly stable. Longitudinal data are needed to assess the extent to which the elderly are coping with illness and disability and the medical, social, and economic factors associated with moving from the community to institutions.

With the growing number of very old persons, it is clear that a strategy for long-term care must be developed to meet the multiple needs of the growing number of elderly at risk for disabling chronic conditions. Any such strategy should include a full range of health and social services covering the long-term continuum from home- and community-based care to institutionalization.[41] It should also provide for the needs of the significant nonelderly population that requires functional assistance.

A variety of critical public policy issues emerge from our examination of chronic illness, disability, and increasing longevity and present challenges to the nation's health sector and to society as a whole. The papers in this volume constitute an important step toward better understanding of these issues.

Notes

1. Saad Z. Nagi, "Some Conceptual Issues in Disability and Rehabilitation," in M. B. Sussman, ed., *Sociology and Rehabilitation* (Washington, D.C.: American Sociological Association, 1965); Lawrence Haber, "Identifying the Disabled: Concepts and Methods in the Measurement of Disability," *Social Security Survey of the Disabled: 1966* (December 1967); Phillip H. N. Wood, "The

Language of Disablement: A Glossary Relating to Disease and Its Consequences," *International Rehabilitation Medicine*, vol. 2, no. 2 (1980), pp. 86–92; World Health Organization, *International Classification of Impairments, Disabilities, and Handicaps* (Geneva, 1980); and World Health Organization, *The Uses of Epidemiology in the Study of the Elderly: Report of a WHO Scientific Group on the Epidemiology of Aging*, Technical Report Series 706 (Geneva, 1984).

2. World Health Organization, *Uses of Epidemiology*, p. 53.

3. Robert H. Brook, John E. Ware, Jr., et al., "Conceptualization and Measurement of Health for Adults in the Health Insurance Study," *Medical Care* (July 1979), vol. 8, *Overview*.

4. Saad Z. Nagi, "An Epidemiology of Disability among Adults in the United States," *Milbank Memorial Fund Quarterly* (Fall 1976), pp. 439–67.

5. Mordechai E. Lando, Richard R. Cutler, and Edward Gamber, *1978 Survey of Disability and Work—Data Book*, SSA Pub. no. 13-11745 (Social Security Administration, September 1982).

6. Steven H. Chapman, Mitchell P. LaPlante, and Gail Wilensky, "Life Expectancy and Health Status of the Aged," *Social Security Bulletin* (October 1986), pp. 24–48.

7. Kenneth G. Manton, "Changing Concepts of Morbidity and Mortality in the Elderly Population," *Milbank Memorial Fund Quarterly* (Spring 1982), pp. 183–244.

8. National Center for Health Statistics, *Health, United States, 1986*, DHHS Pub. no. (PHS) 87-1232, December 1986, table 12, p. 84.

9. National Center for Health Statistics, "Births, Marriages, Divorces, and Deaths for 1985," *Monthly Vital Statistics Report*, vol. 34, no. 12, DHHS Pub. no. (PHS) 86-1120, March 24, 1986.

10. National Center for Health Statistics, "Current Estimates from the National Health Interview Survey, United States, 1985," *Vital and Health Statistics*, Series 10, no. 160, DHHS Pub. no. (PHS) 86-1588, September 1986.

11. U.S. Bureau of the Census, "Projections of the Population of the United States, by Age, Sex, and Race: 1983 to 2080," *Current Population Reports*, Series P-25, no. 952, May 1984.

12. National Center for Health Statistics, "Current Estimates, 1985," p. 138.

13. International Center for the Disabled, *The ICD Survey of Disabled Americans: Bringing Disabled Americans into the Mainstream*, March 1986.

14. Candace L. Macken, "A Profile of Functionally Impaired Elderly Persons Living in the Community," *Health Care Financing Review* (Summer 1986), pp. 33–49.

15. Lando et al., *1978 Survey of Disability and Work*.

16. National Center for Health Statistics, "Health Characteristics of Persons with Chronic Activity Limitations: United States, 1979," *Vital and Health Statistics*, Series 10, no. 137, DHHS Pub. no. (PHS) 82-1565, December 1981.

17. National Center for Health Statistics, "Americans Needing Home Care, United States," *Vital and Health Statistics*, Series 10, no. 153, DHHS Pub. no. (PHS) 86-1581, March 1986.

18. James F. Fries, "Aging, Natural Death, and the Compression of Morbidity," *New England Journal of Medicine*, July 17, 1980, pp. 130–35.

19. Morton Kramer, "The Rising Pandemic of Mental Disorders and Associated Chronic Diseases and Disorders," *Acta Psychiatrica Scandinavica*, supplement 185, vol. 62 (1980), pp. 382–96.

20. Ernest M. Gruenberg, "The Failures of Success," *Milbank Memorial Fund Quarterly* (Winter 1977), pp. 3–24.

21. Edward L. Schneider and Jacob A. Brody, "Aging, Natural Death, and the Compression of Morbidity: Another View," *New England Journal of Medicine*, October 6, 1983, pp. 854–56.

22. Manton, "Changing Concepts of Morbidity and Mortality."

23. Dorothy P. Rice and Jacob J. Feldman, "Living Longer in the United States: Demographic Changes and Health Needs of the Elderly," *Milbank Memorial Fund Quarterly* (Summer 1983), pp. 362–96.

24. Lois M. Verbrugge, "Longer Life but Worsening Health? Trends in Health and Mortality of Middle-aged and Older Persons," *Milbank Memorial Fund Quarterly* (Fall 1984), pp. 475–519.

25. Ronald W. Wilson and Thomas F. Drury, "Interpreting Trends in Illness and Disability: Health Statistics and Health Status," *Annual Review of Public Health*, no. 5 (1984), pp. 83–106.

26. Thomas N. Chirikos, "Accounting for the Historical Rise in Work Disability Prevalence," *Milbank Quarterly*, no. 2 (1986), pp. 271–301.

27. Jonathan Sunshine, "Disability Payments Stabilizing after Era of Accelerating Growth," *Monthly Labor Review* (May 1981), pp. 17–22.

28. John W. Rowe, "Health Care of the Elderly," *New England Journal of Medicine*, March 28, 1985, pp. 827–35; and Kenneth G. Manton, "Future Patterns of Chronic Disease Incidence, Disability, and Mortality among the Elderly: Implications for the Demand for Acute and Long-Term Health Care," *New York State Journal of Medicine* (November 1985), pp. 623–33.

29. Edward H. Yelin, Jane S. Kramer, and Wallace V. Epstein, "Arthritis Policy and the Elderly," Policy Paper no. 5, Aging Health Policy Center, University of California, San Francisco, 1983.

30. Paul W. Newacheck, Peter P. Budetti, and Neal Halfon, "Trends in Activity-limiting Chronic Conditions among Children," *American Journal of Public Health* (February 1986), pp. 178–84.

31. Jacob J. Feldman, "Work Ability of the Aged under Conditions of Improving Mortality," *Milbank Memorial Fund Quarterly* (Summer 1983), pp. 430–44; Verbrugge, "Longer Life but Worsening Health?"; and Chirikos, "Accounting for the Historical Rise."

32. Chapman, LaPlante, and Wilensky, "Life Expectancy and Health Status."

33. National Center for Health Statistics, "Utilization of Short-Stay Hospitals: Annual Summary for the United States, 1980," *Vital and Health Statistics*, Series 13, no. 64, DHHS Pub. no. (PHS) 82-1725, March 1982, p. 2.

34. Lu Ann Aday, Gretchen V. Fleming, and Ronald Andersen, *Access to Medical Care in the U.S.: Who Has It, Who Doesn't* (Chicago: Pluribus Press, 1984).

35. National Center for Health Statistics, "Net Difference in Interview Data

on Chronic Conditions and Information Derived from Medical Records," Series 2, no. 57, DHEW Pub. no. (HRA) 76-1331, June 1973.

36. National Center for Health Statistics, "Interview Data on Chronic Conditions Compared with Information Derived from Medical Records," *Vital and Health Statistics*, Series 2, no. 23, May 1967.

37. Brenda C. Cox and Steven B. Cohen, *Methodological Issues for Health Surveys* (New York: Marcel Dekker, 1985), chap. 6, pp. 150–89.

38. Mordechai E. Lando, Alice V. Farley, and Mary A. Brown, "Recent Trends in the Social Security Disability Insurance Program," *Social Security Bulletin*, vol. 45, no. 8 (August 1982), pp. 3–14.

39. James Lubitz and Penelope Pine, "Health Care Use by Medicare's Disabled Enrollees," *Health Care Financing Review*, vol. 7, no. 4 (Summer 1986), pp. 19–31.

40. Constance W. Mahoney, Carroll L. Estes, and Judith E. Heumann, *Toward a Unified Agenda: Proceedings of a National Conference on Disability and Aging* (San Francisco: Institute for Health and Aging, University of California, 1986).

41. Dorothy P. Rice and Carroll L. Estes, "Health of the Elderly: Policy Issues and Challenges," *Health Affairs*, vol. 3, no. 4 (Winter 1984), pp. 25–49.

3
Financing Long-Term Care: A Major Obstacle to Reform

Judith W. Meltzer

More than ten years have passed since the health policy community identified the provision of long-term care services for the elderly and disabled as a priority issue. In the early 1970s, "long-term care" was a relatively new term, meaning different things to different people. To many, it simply meant nursing home care; to others, it meant anything *but* nursing home care; and to a few, it carried the meaning most of us have now come to accept—that is, meeting the full range of health, social, personal care, and housing needs of individuals, both elderly and disabled, who require assistance over an extended period of time with some or all activities of daily living.

Ten years ago, analysts concerned about long-term care predicted that demand would begin to increase dramatically in the 1980s, reaching a peak in the years 2000 to 2030. Many argued the importance of planning for a more rational system of financing, managing, and providing services in order to be prepared for the inevitable increases in need that would accompany an aging U.S. population. Progress has occurred in the past decade, both in our understanding of the problems confronting those who need long-term care and in research and development of service systems to reach people in need. But it is also true that we are nowhere near having developed an acceptable public policy for long-term care.

Almost every administration since Richard Nixon's has tried to develop a coherent policy for long-term care. In the recent past, there have been several national task force efforts, many congressional hearings, and a lot of talk about long-term care. What has emerged is an implicit consensus on some of the basic elements of a system of long-term care; for example, greater reliance on community and in-home services, deemphasis of the medical model, and the desirability of local case management. There is, however, one critical thing missing from this consensus that is a major obstacle to the future development of policy for long-term care: a strategy for financing long-term care services. Without a financing plan and a willingness to redirect financial resources to assistance for long-term care, we will continue to have an imbalance between needs and the availability of services for both the elderly and the adult disabled populations.

This chapter focuses on questions related to the financing of long-term care, first briefly describing current public and private financing with emphasis on the major federal and state programs offering assistance for long-term care. This is followed by a discussion of several unresolved issues in the development of a financing strategy. The chapter concludes by suggesting several targets of opportunity for future policy development.

Current Financing of Long-Term Care

Current financing of services for long-term care comes from many public and private sources. Although it is not possible to estimate total costs accurately, approximately 60 to 80 percent of long-term care services are provided informally by friends, neighbors, and relatives without payment.[1] Public expenditures for long-term care, of which approximately three-quarters goes to support nursing home care, are still quite substantial, amounting to about $20 billion in 1985. Government expenditures account for 44 percent of all nursing home payments; the remainder come from private sources, 97 percent of which are direct out-of-pocket payments by consumers.[2]

Government assistance is scattered among eighty federal programs and countless state and local initiatives that support long-term care services, either directly through payment for care or indirectly through income transfers and provision of in-kind services.[3]

Table 3–1 describes five major federal programs supporting long-term care services. They are Medicaid (Title XIX of the Social Security Act); Medicare (Title XVIII of the Social Security Act); the Social Services Block Grant (Title XX of the Social Security Act); Title III of the Older Americans Act; and the Supplemental Security Income program (Title XVI of the Social Security Act). Not included in the table but also significant are the Veterans Administration nursing care and domiciliary care programs, Department of Housing and Urban Development (HUD) programs supporting congregate housing for the elderly and handicapped, and funds for independent living centers for the disabled provided by Title VII of the Rehabilitation Act.

Despite the large number of programs providing some assistance, most public support comes from only one source—the

TABLE 3-1
Major Federal Programs Supporting Long-Term Care Services

Program	Services Covered	Eligibility	Administering Agency Federal	Administering Agency State
Medicaid (Title XIX of the Social Security Act)	Skilled nursing facility[a] Intermediate care facility[b] Home health[c] Adult day care[b]	Aged, blind, disabled persons receiving cash assistance under Supplemental Security Income (SSI); others receiving cash assistance under Aid to Families with Dependent Children (AFDC). At state option, persons whose incomes exceed standards for cash assistance under SSI/AFDC (the "medically needy")	Health Care Financing Administration/ HHS	State Medicaid agency
	2176 "waiver" services: case management, homemaker, personal care, adult day care, habilitation, respite, and other services at state option[d]	Aged, blind, disabled, or mentally ill Medicaid eligibles (including children) living in the community who would require nursing home care. At state option, persons living in the community with higher income than normally allowed under a state Medicaid plan		In some cases, the 2176 "waiver" program may be administered by another agency, such as the state agency on aging

Medicare (Title XVIII of the Social Security Act)	100 days of skilled nursing facility care Home health care Hospice care	Generally, social security status. Persons 65 and over; persons under 65 entitled to federal disability benefits; and certain persons with end-stage renal disease	Health Care Financing Administration/HHS	NA
Social Services Block Grant (Title XX of the Social Security Act)	Various social services as defined by the state, including homemaker assistance, home health aide, personal care, home-delivered meals	No federal requirements. States may require means test	Office of Human Development Services/HHS	State social services/human resources agency. In some cases other state agencies such as the state agency on aging may administer a portion of Title XX funds for certain groups

(Table continues)

TABLE 3–1 (continued)

Program	Services Covered	Eligibility	Administering Agency	
			Federal	State
Older Americans Act (Title III)	Variety of social services as determined by state and area agencies on aging, with priority on in-home services. Case management, day care, protective services. Separate appropriation for home-delivered meals	Persons 60 and over. No means tests, but services are to be targeted to those with social or economic need	Administration on Aging/Office of Human Development Services/HHS	State agency on aging

Supplemental Security Income (Title XVI of the Social Security Act)	Federal income support. Maximum payment for person with no income was $340 per individual and $510 per couple in 1987. Supplemental payment for nonmedical housing or in-home services, as determined by state	Aged, blind, disabled persons who meet federally established income and resources requirements. States may make payments to other state-defined eligibility groups	Social Security Administration/ HHS	State supplemental payment program may be federally administered or state administered (usually by the public assistance agency)

a. Required for individuals over age twenty-one.
b. At option of state.
c. Required for individuals entitled to skilled nursing home care.
d. May be offered under a waiver of Medicaid state plan requirements if requested by the state and approved by the Department of Health and Human Services (HHS). May include waiver of Medicaid eligibility requirements and stipulation that services be offered statewide.

SOURCE: Congressional Research Service, Library of Congress.

federal-state Medicaid program. Medicaid pays primarily for nursing home care in skilled nursing facilities (SNFs) and intermediate care facilities (ICFs), although a small but growing amount of Medicaid funds supports home health services. In addition, in the Omnibus Budget Reconciliation Act of 1981, Congress created the Section 2176 home- and community-based services waiver program. This legislation allows states to waive certain Medicaid requirements in order to provide home- and community-based services to Medicaid-eligible clients at risk of institutionalization. Forty-seven states have used this authority to set up expanded programs of community care for the elderly, the physically disabled, and the mentally retarded and developmentally disabled (MR-DD) populations as alternatives to nursing home care. Table 3–2 shows FY 1985 Medicaid expenditures for long-term care services.

Medicaid alone accounts for about 43 percent of total national spending for nursing home care. Further, payments for long-term care services consume 47 percent of all federal and state Medicaid dollars. Medicaid's dominant part in the public financing of long-term care may seem surprising in light of its original purpose and structure. Enacted in 1965 as a program to provide health care protection for the poor, Medicaid's mission has been increasingly redirected to long-term care. Its current role as the principal public supporter of long-term care is problematic in many ways; the burden of long-term care expenditures inhibits states' capacities to meet the basic health care needs of the poor fully; at the same time, Medicaid's eligibility and benefit restrictions often have serious negative consequences for recipients of long-term care. To be eligible for Medicaid benefits,

TABLE 3–2

MEDICAID EXPENDITURES FOR LONG-TERM CARE
(FEDERAL AND STATE), FISCAL YEAR 1985
(billions of dollars)

Service	Expenditures
Skilled nursing facilities (SNFs)	5.06
Intermediate care facilities (ICFs)	6.5
Intermediate care facilities for mentally retarded (ICF-MRs)	4.7
Home health care	1.1
Section 2176 home- and community-based services	0.3
Total long-term care	17.66
Total Medicaid expenditures	37.5
Long-term care as percentage of total Medicaid	47

SOURCE: Health Care Financing Administration.

individuals must be impoverished. Because Medicaid is a federal-state program, eligibility levels vary greatly from state to state. In general, however, Medicaid recipients must be very poor (have incomes below the poverty level) or spend all of their existing resources on medical or nursing home care. Many individuals enter nursing homes as paying clients but very quickly exhaust all their resources and become eligible for Medicaid financing.

The Medicare program, which provides health insurance for the elderly and disabled, offers extremely limited benefits for long-term care, contrary to the perception of the overwhelming majority of the elderly, who assume that Medicare will protect them if they need long-term nursing care. In fact, Medicare provides only very limited skilled nursing facility and home care benefits, both of which are even further restricted by federal regulations governing the need for care and the conditions under which payment will be made. Medicare regulations have defined eligibility for both nursing home and home health care benefits in such restrictive ways that they are available only for short periods of time for post–acute health care needs.[4] As a result, Medicare benefits for skilled nursing and home health care combined total only about $2.5 billion, or 4 percent of total Medicare spending.[5] It is interesting to note, however, that the Medicare home health benefit is the fastest growing part of the Medicare program.

A third but often overlooked source of financing for long-term care is the Supplemental Security Income (SSI) program, which provides a national minimum income for elderly and disabled Americans. In January 1986 SSI provided a maximum monthly benefit of $336 for an eligible individual and $503 for a couple with no other income. In addition, the basic federal grant is supplemented by about two-thirds of the states for individuals living independently and for those in group living arrangements. These supplements for group living or domiciliary care facilities are significant for long-term care policy. Currently, about 5 percent of the SSI caseload, or 226,000 persons, live in nonmedical domiciliary facilities such as board and care homes. State supplements for domiciliary and attendant care totaled about $400 million in 1982. The use of SSI payments for domiciliary and board and care homes presents another difficult policy problem. The SSI program, by law, provides cash payments to individuals rather than payments to providers. As a result, it has been very difficult for the federal government and even for state governments to enforce licensing standards and to regulate the quality of care provided in these facilities.

Private financing for long-term care consists mostly of direct out-of-pocket payments by clients and their families. Although private sector financing alternatives such as insurance for long-term care and life-care communities are attractive, existing private initiatives reach only small numbers of people. Despite expressions of interest by the insurance industry, only about thirty insurance companies offer long-term care policies covering elderly persons. Surveys estimate that these policies cover 50,000 to 150,000 persons.[6] The typical insurance coverage offered by these few companies is also fairly limited, usually providing indemnity coverage for a fixed number of days of nursing home care, often with high deductibles, waiting periods, and exclusions.[7]

Life-care communities are housing developments that offer elderly residents a range of housing alternatives, activities, and long-term care services as their needs for assistance grow. Residents pay a large lump-sum entrance fee and monthly charges in exchange for receiving services for the rest of their lives. Many life-care communities offer housing alternatives ranging from independent apartments to congregate living arrangements to skilled nursing homes and provide meals, homemaking help, personal care, and a range of medical and nonmedical services. Estimates of the number of life-care communities nationwide range from 275 to 600, serving about 90,000 residents. Their number is growing rapidly, however, and the American Association of Retired Persons has estimated that they will double during the next decade.[8] But because of the large entrance fee— often as high as $100,000—they are marketed to the affluent elderly and affect only a small proportion of those likely to need long-term care services.

Problems and Issues in Financing Long-Term Care

Several issues must be resolved in developing financing strategies for long-term care. This discussion is not an exhaustive analysis of problems with the current provision of care; but it goes beyond strict financing questions, because the method of paying for care is integrally tied to the delivery system.

Public versus Private Support for Long-Term Care. Three things are obvious when looking at current expenditures. First, a lot of public money is already spent for long-term care services; second, current expenditures are not sufficient to meet current and anticipated needs; and third, government alone cannot shoulder all of the costs of care for the populations at risk. The questions that must be resolved are how much government should pay for, for whom it should pay, and under what circumstances.

A related question concerns how much we can expect from the private sector—from individuals and their families and from risk-sharing initiatives like private long-term care insurance. Recent interest in stimulating private insurance and in tax and other strategies to enhance individuals' ability to finance their own care stems from the hope that expanded private capacity will relieve some of the burden now felt by public programs. The most recent expression of this interest is HHS Secretary Otis Bowen's proposal for tax incentives to encourage individuals to save money and companies to offer insurance covering long-term care. These are desirable goals. Early analysis, however, provides only hints of the promise of private initiatives. There is a real danger that concern about public spending and rhetoric about the capacity of the private sector will lead to overstated expectations.[9] Despite some recent increases in the availability of insurance policies that cover services for long-term care, it is uncertain whether they will ever be widely available and affordable for significant numbers of elderly and disabled persons.

Proposals to encourage increased savings for long-term care through individual retirement accounts, for example, assume that individuals can be persuaded to plan for future and uncertain needs. These proposals, and life-care communities, are targeted to moderate-to high-income elderly persons, and not to those elderly living in or near poverty. Reverse-annuity mortgages (RAMs), although an intellectually intriguing idea, have yet to show practical effects. RAMs allow elderly people to convert the equity in their homes into cash they can use for health care and other long-term care. It has been estimated that elderly homeowners have an average equity of more than $50,000 in their homes.[10] Despite convincing analytic arguments, however, RAMs have not become widespread. Fewer than 600 of them have been written in the entire country, and it appears that many elderly persons are unwilling to remortgage their most substantial financial asset.

All of this is not to say that private initiatives should not be pursued, but to caution that they be put in proper perspective. What we need is not a public versus private dichotomy, but an attempt to strike the right balance and partnership between the two. We might reasonably expect the private sector to offer added protections to individuals in the middle and on the upper end of the income scale, but it is misleading to suggest that in their *current* state of development they will significantly reduce the public burden or responsibility. Part of the challenge for the future is to find ways to construct private sector alternatives so that they are applicable to greater portions of the at-risk population. For example, can public incentives be developed to help create a market for private insurance, and can insurance policies be structured so that their costs are less prohibitive? These are currently unanswered but extremely important questions.

The Unprotected Middle Class. Reliance on Medicaid financing as the major public support for long-term care means that individuals must be impoverished to be eligible for assistance. Although states have made some changes in eligibility in their Section 2176 waiver programs, these are generally small demonstration efforts to offer in-home and community services to defined populations of persons at risk of institutional care. In most states, therefore, few means are available to help individuals whose social security benefits and other income put them slightly above the poverty level. For many persons who could remain at home with a small amount of home-based care, the only answer is to get sick enough to require nursing home care, use their savings and other assets to "spend down" to the Medicaid eligibility levels, and then become permanent Medicaid clients. This is a particular hardship on couples whose well spouse is forced into poverty in order to secure care for the spouse requiring it.

"Medicalization" of Financing for Long-Term Care. The medical/institutional bias in the financing of long-term care has long been recognized. With the exception of the Section 2176 waiver programs, almost all current programs support care in medically based institutions, even though we know that many individuals' needs are not strictly medical. The difficulty is in searching for financing alternatives that reduce the medical bias. Medicaid is clearly not the right mechanism to finance long-term care services, but it exists and it is open-ended, meaning that states are reimbursed according to a matching ratio for all allowable expenditures they make on behalf of eligible clients. Despite repeated efforts by the Reagan administration to "cap" the program (that is, eliminate the open-ended matching), Medicaid remains one of the few programs with the capacity to expand somewhat with increasing needs.

The dilemma is glaringly apparent when one looks at the growth in funding for intermediate care facilities for the mentally retarded (ICF-MRs). Advocates of care for the mentally retarded and developmentally disabled admit that institutional care is an undesirable alternative and have pursued legislative strategies to reduce the size and medical orientation of ICF-MRs. At the same time, they are not willing to restructure the financing to restrict Medicaid's open-ended payment for existing care, believing that an imperfect ICF-MR benefit with its inflexible service design is preferable to a restricted community care grant. They are uncomfortable about a trade-off that would allow for a broader range of services but that is more likely to be underfunded and unable to grow with increased needs.

How to Balance the Needs for Acute and Long-Term Care. Related to medicalization of care is the question of balancing the acute and long-term care needs of the elderly and disabled populations. The proper provision of care should meet both needs, but the question is whether both kinds of care should be financed and provided through the same or different programs.

Currently, Medicare pays for acute care for the elderly and disabled. Medicaid pays for some acute care needs of the low-income elderly and disabled, acting as a public "Medi-gap" policy, and also pays for long-term care. Medicaid, as the payer of last resort, is heavily affected by what Medicare will and will not pay for. The relationship between the two is exemplified by the often-heard quip, "When Medicare sneezes, Medicaid gets a cold." A further complication is that the programs are administered at different levels of government. Most state Medicaid agencies, for example, will try to secure Medicare funding before initiating payment for skilled nursing or home health services. As Medicare continues to tighten its eligibility and benefit payments, pressures on Medicaid increase.

In considering new financing strategies, the question is whether to combine or separate financing for acute and long-term care for at-risk populations. One strategy, proposed by the National Study Group on State Medicaid Strategies, advocates taking long-term care out of the Medicaid program and establishing a separate continuing care system for the financing and provision of long-term care. This proposal would make the long-term care program distinct from Medicare's and Medicaid's provision of acute care benefits.[11]

Others argue that separating acute and long-term care will exacerbate current problems of fragmentation. They argue for integrating the financing system to stimulate the development of delivery systems that meet all of the needs of the populations served.[12] They believe that only by combining financing for acute and long-term care can we provide the incentives to get people out of hospitals and nursing homes and force the necessary financial trade-offs between expensive acute care and less expensive personal care and social services. Social/HMO experiments are based on the premise that it is desirable to integrate the financing and delivery of acute care, institutional chronic care, and community-based social support. The social/HMO concept being tested at several sites around the country includes hospitalization, home-based long-term care, and medical and social services in a single capitated system, meaning that one agency is responsible and at risk for providing this comprehensive range of long-term care services to an enrolled population.

Income Supplementation versus Payments to Providers. The basic question here is whether new strategies for financing long-term care should emphasize supplementing beneficiaries' incomes or making direct payments to providers. Existing financing is heavily weighted toward fee-for-service payments to providers. But as we move away from a medical/institutional model of care, income supplementation strategies may become more popular.

Income supplementation means granting additional income or buying power to persons needing long-term care and, in some cases, to family members and other informal care givers. Whereas current financing is linked to providers of specific services, an income strategy gives direct control of the resources to purchase care to consumers of care. The disabled have argued for a greater emphasis on cash payments as a means of increasing their autonomy and independence in seeking and getting needed care.

Income strategies for long-term care can take several forms. One might be a direct cash supplement to a functionally impaired person to pay for the costs of care. One way of providing this would be to supplement an existing income support program, such as SSI, on the basis of some prior determination of both the severity of the disability and the need for long-term care services. Another form of income supplementation would be a tax subsidy in the form of either a deduction or a refundable credit for family members who provide care for an elderly and disabled person in their home or in the elderly person's home. The tax subsidy could be an incentive for families to provide care by granting them financial support to cover the costs. A third type of income strategy would be to issue vouchers to pay for long-term care. A voucher could be implemented through a new service-oriented system.

An income supplementation strategy could enhance the control and autonomy of consumers of care and provide greater incentives for informal and family care giving. A disadvantage, however, is that additional income will not by itself help restructure the delivery system except to the extent that services are developed to match consumer demand. Further, it is difficult to envision income supplements large enough to cover costs for individuals requiring full-time or specialized nursing services. It should be possible, however, to develop strategies that combine payments to providers for some types

JUDITH W. MELTZER

of care with income supplements to pay for personal care, supportive housing alternatives, or other services for which greater client control is desirable.

The Elderly versus the Disabled. The phrase long-term care is generally used in reference to care of the elderly. But there is another group that needs and uses the services of long-term care, and these are disabled persons. Individuals who have chronic and serious mental and physical disabilities often need various kinds of assistance to enable them to realize their fullest potential in the least restrictive environment. This assistance can be classified as long-term care.

Elderly and disabled persons requiring long-term care have many similar needs, but there are also key differences. In looking at financing and delivery alternatives, the issue of whether to design unified or parallel programs for the elderly and disabled must be decided. The principles embodied in the disability rights movement and the desire of the disabled for opportunities for independent living can make a substantial contribution to the reform of long-term care for the elderly as well as for the disabled. The values held by those at the forefront of the disability rights movement are often the same ones held by the elderly, although perhaps expressed in different words. Like the disabled, most elderly persons prefer to stay in their own homes rather than be institutionalized in nursing homes or other large facilities. Like the disabled, elderly people prefer to socialize with people of all ages instead of being segregated on the basis of their age. Many elderly persons want to be able to continue working past age sixty-five. And probably the majority of people over age sixty-five prefer making their own decisions to relying on professionals.

Thus disabled and elderly persons have some very similar preferences. Senior citizens and their advocates, however, have not made as compelling a case as disabled people that self-direction and autonomy are essential elements of a system of long-term care.

Although much of the emphasis in discussions of long-term care policy is on the elderly, similar consideration must be given to the needs of physically and mentally disabled adults and of the MR-DD populations. The basic questions remain the same—how to finance and organize care and deliver it efficiently. Each of the subgroups of the population needing long-term care has, to some extent, developed its own professionals, delivery systems, and advocates. In the future, we must decide if these parallel systems should be joined or if it makes more sense to organize services around the subgroups of the population in need.

How to Ration Public Resources Equitably. A final issue that any financing strategy must address is how to "ration" limited public resources—how to decide which people are eligible for what kinds of public support and how to distribute available resources for long-term care equitably among them. A related question is how much of the burden of long-term care should be borne by government and how much by individuals and family members.

Existing strategies for rationing public resources all have serious flaws. Although focusing resources universally on a target population, that is, on the elderly or the disabled, is conceptually clean and easy to administer, it does not allow for discrimination based on level of need. But it is not simple to determine who is most in need. An argument can be made for basing the determination on functional need, with the most seriously limited persons getting helped first, or on financial need, with the poorest first—or on some combination of the two. The problem is further complicated by the existence or absence of familial supports. If, for example, two individuals show equal need based on functional limitation but one has a spouse who provides care and the other lives alone, should the public assessment of "need" focus only on the solitary individual? This decision becomes even more difficult when an assessment of need is tied to eligibility for public support.

Clearly, resource constraints will require that these types of decisions be made. Fiscal pressures will also necessitate other rationing devices, such as means tests based on ability to pay, copayment mechanisms to reduce use, and eligibility restrictions based on severity of need to target services to those with the most severe or debilitating problems.

Hope for the Future

This is where the long-term care discussion usually ends. Armed with an understanding of the problems and an appreciation of the very difficult and complex issues that must be resolved, analysts and politicians alike begin to wonder if anything can be done. It is not the purpose of this chapter to lay out definitive solutions, but several conclusions can be drawn from the analysis.

First, public support for long-term care assistance must be expanded and changed. Existing financing mechanisms are inadequate and ill suited to the problems of the elderly and disabled needing long-term care. Next, although the development of private initiatives should be encouraged and supported, we must be careful not to overstate their potential by themselves. It would be a mistake to assume that private insurance for long-term care, for example, will one day obviate the need for a large public investment. The goal should not be the privatization of long-term care; rather, we must seek ways to develop productive partnerships between private and public resources so that each can be used more appropriately and efficiently.

Finally, it is unlikely that any one public financing strategy will be developed in the near term to replace and improve the existing conglomeration of programs. Thus, efforts must be directed to strengthening and making more rational those programs that are now in place. This means redoubling efforts to expand the Medicaid home- and community-based waiver projects, supporting SSI expansions— particularly those aimed at income supplementation for domiciliary care—and finding new resources to expand the availability of personal care services and supportive housing arrangements. Ten years ago we talked about planning to meet the long-term care needs of the 1980s and 1990s. Unfortunately, the future is now, and much remains to be done.

Notes

1. Study Group on State Medicaid Strategies, *Long-Term Care*, Background Papers, no. 3 (Washington, D.C.: Center for the Study of Social Policy, January 1984), p. 91.

2. Carol O'Shaughnessy, Richard Price, and Jeanne Griffith, "Financing and Delivery of Long-Term Care Services for the Elderly," Congressional Research Service, Library of Congress, February 24, 1987, p. ix.

3. Ibid., p. 19.

4. To be eligible for home health care, for example, clients must be "homebound," their care needs must be "intermittent," and they must have a need for daily skilled nursing care. These provisions severely restrict who can get home health care under Medicare.

5. Judith Feder, testimony before the Subcommittee on Health and the Environment, Committee on Energy and Commerce, U.S. House of Representatives, October 18, 1985.

6. O'Shaughnessy et al., "Financing and Delivery of Long-Term Care," p. 57.

7. Douglas Nelson, "Financing the Future of Long-Term Care: An Overview and Direction for Change," Working Paper, Center for the Study of Social Policy, Washington, D.C., August 1986, p. 21.

8. Ann Trueblood Raper, ed., *National Continuing Care Directory* (Washington, D.C.: American Association of Retired Persons, 1984), p. 5.

9. Judith Feder and William Scanlon, "Problems and Prospects in Financing Long-Term Care," Center for Health Policy Studies, Georgetown University, Washington, D.C., December 1985.

10. "Home Equity Financing of Long-Term Care for the Elderly," statement by Bruce Jacobs and William Weissert (Hearings before the Subcommittee on Health, Committee on Finance, U.S. Senate, November 13–14, 1984).

11. See National Study Group on State Medicaid Strategies, "Restructuring Medicaid: An Agenda for Change," Center for the Study of Social Policy, Washington, D.C., January 1984.

12. Stanley Wallack, testimony before the Senate Subcommittee on Health, Committee on Finance, November 1983, pp. 216–19.

4

Is Medical Care
the Right Prescription
for Chronic Illness?

Arthur L. Caplan

Chronic illness and disability are much-discussed topics in the world of health policy. Arguments rage as to whether the nation's population is growing sicker as it grows older.[1] It certainly seems that more people who in previous decades would have died from congenital conditions, injuries, or severe illnesses are now being kept alive but with varying degrees of impairment and morbidity. It is commonly noted that the price of successful acute care medical interventions is a population that will live longer but be sicker.

Economists, politicians, and the occasional physician seem to take a perverse delight in proffering Cassandra-like forecasts of an America overwhelmed by the demands of the aged, the diseased, and the disabled. The practitioners of the dismal science are living up to their name by engaging in a somewhat unseemly competition to see who can issue the most doleful assessment, the direst warning about the imminent insolvency of Medicare, social security, and special federal programs such as the Veterans Administration hospital system. Professional wisdom has it that these programs will soon be awash in a torrent of chronically ill and disabled persons who will in turn drown them in a sea of red ink.[2]

In the context of these hotly contested political and policy debates, it might seem naive if not downright stupid to suggest that the issues raised by chronic illness and disability require ethical rather than economic analysis for their resolution. Nonetheless, I believe that this is so. Answers to the questions of how much should be spent on the chronically ill and disabled, what priority ought to be accorded

The author would like to acknowledge the support of the Henry Luce Foundation in the preparation of this paper.

policies aimed at helping those who are chronically ill or disabled, and what goals should guide health care interventions directed at these populations depend on the ethical weight that is accorded chronic illness and disability.

Perhaps the major question requiring critical reflection is whether chronic illness ought be understood as a category or type of illness in itself. Do disability and chronic illness bear important similarities to acute illness? If not, they may require different responses from patients, health care providers, and policy makers.

If chronic illness does not require the same response from society as acute illness and if the services sought and needed are different, then the consequences for social policy and fiscal solvency may be different as well. Only if chronic illness and disability fit—or are forced to fit—into the prevailing conceptual framework for treating and paying for acute disease do increases in the proportion of chronically ill and disabled need to keep so many of those charged with balancing local, state, and federal budgets awake at night.

What Is the Relationship between Acute and Chronic Conditions?

If chronic illness and disability differ in no important respects from acute illness or injury and are merely diseases that afflict a person over an extended period of time, then deciding how much should be spent to help the chronically ill and disabled will require nothing new to be added to existing debates about equity and justice in the domain of health care. Chronic illness and injuries, as well as genetic anomalies capable of producing long-term impairment or dysfunction, while differing in degree from acute illness, would not be different in kind.

Those who have disabling pain, chronic arthritis, or chronic emphysema would gain or lose little in their efforts to secure a share of the resources available for health care by noting that their afflictions are permanent and incurable. The fact that a medical problem persists over time might increase the needs of the chronically ill and disabled relative to those of others with medical problems, but it would mean nothing in terms of the moral weight assigned to the needs of those with chronic or incurable disabling conditions.

If the chronically ill and disabled are concerned with securing a greater share of the nation's health care resources, they might indeed be happy to have their conditions treated as possessing the same moral weight as bacterial meningitis, a myocardial infarction, a sudden severe depression, a gunshot wound, or other dramatic examples of acute injury and illness. The treatment of acute illness and injury dominates the organization of our health care system, the educational orientation of our academic medical centers, the norms that guide interventions by health care professionals in hospital and other institutional settings, and the kinds of regulatory and reimbursement schemes that have evolved for treating illness and disease.[3] Simply viewing chronic illness and disability as a subcategory of illness and disease generally, therefore, would require a drastic revision in both clinical and societal policies concerning the allocation of health care resources to the chronically ill and disabled.

Advocates of the chronically ill and disabled are well aware of this fact. A great deal of the political advocacy on behalf of the chronically ill and disabled focuses on the similarity of their needs to the needs of those with acute illnesses. The language of equal rights is much in evidence when advocates for the disabled and the chronically ill present their case in Washington or in the various state capitals.[4]

The case for lumping disabilities and chronic conditions in with acute and emergency medical problems is based on the premise that our society seems willing to recognize the moral claim generated by the needs of those with life-threatening illnesses. The push to create a program of insurance to cover the costs of catastrophic illness within the Medicare program illustrates the moral power of acute medical problems in commanding scarce federal dollars. Since needs for acute medical care can generate societal obligations to satisfy these needs in the context of a hospital emergency room, as many have observed,[5] it would seem the most effective political strategy for those trying to secure resources for the chronically ill and disabled to draw analogies between these conditions and acute, life-threatening diseases.

This strategy might, in fact, be practical for obtaining more resources than are now being allotted for the needs of the chronically ill and disabled. Chronic illnesses and disabilities have not evoked the same degree of concern as acute, life-threatening illnesses. On first inspection, therefore, there might appear to be no benefit in distinguishing between acute and chronic medical problems.

The inadvisability of drawing any sharp distinctions between acute and chronic health care needs is further reinforced by the well-known aversion of insurance companies, the federal government, and other third parties to paying for those with chronic medical problems. Such attitudes are not unique to reimbursement programs. Prepaid health plans such as health maintenance organizations (HMOs) and preferred provider organizations (PPOs) are notoriously reluctant to assume the financial costs of chronic illness and disability. Our financing schemes for reimbursing the costs of illness are oriented toward acute episodes of disease, precise categories of diagnosis and treatment (most recently exemplified in the diagnosis-related group—DRG—system used in Medicare's prospective payment scheme), and measurable outcomes of progress and cure. Chronic illness and disability do not fare well under these criteria.

The reason for the relative underfunding of services and institutions aimed at helping those with chronic illnesses and disabilities is also well known. There is a fear that if third-party payers were to cover the costs of disability and chronic conditions they would soon go broke. If chronic illness and disability were treated on a conceptual par with acute illness, there seems to be a very real threat that the chronically ill and disabled—because of their complicated and continuing medical needs—would simply "hijack" all the resources made available for health care or any other social purpose.[6] The fiscal burden that might be created by more generous reimbursement policies for chronic conditions is illustrated by Medicare's only attempt to reimburse the costs of chronic illness—the end-stage renal disease program for those with chronic renal failure.

In 1972 Congress created a special program to cover the costs of dialysis for all who suffered from kidney failure. At the time, the program was expected to cost $200–300 million and to extend benefits to approximately 20,000 people. Today, the end-stage renal disease program pays more than $2 billion to cover the costs of dialysis for more than 80,000 patients.[7] Experts predict increases in both the number of eligible claimants and the amount of money spent for at least another ten years.

The costs of treating chronic renal failure left a searing impression on the minds of policy makers. Avoiding the creation of another program like that for end-stage renal disease has become dogma among many legislators and bureaucrats in Washington.

The threat of injustice in the distribution of resources is the most important political reason for distinguishing between acute and chronic illness. The projected costs of covering nursing home care, outpatient medications, the provision of therapies in the home, and comprehensive care of the handicapped and mentally ill are so large as to make it difficult for politicians to allow disability and chronic illnesses to be considered as deserving as acute illness.

But cost is not the only reason for drawing a distinction between acute and chronic medical problems, nor is it obviously a morally sound reason. If the only thing special about chronic illness and disability is that they are expensive to treat, this in itself is not a particularly impressive basis for drawing sharp distinctions between what we feel obligated to pay for in health care and what we do not. There is another reason to hesitate before arguing that chronic illness and disability merit the same societal concern and fiscal outlays that acute medical problems and emergencies currently receive: possible loss of personal autonomy.

Professional Authority and Individual Autonomy

Acute illness is the province of medicine. Physicians have almost complete sovereignty over diagnosis, treatment, palliation, and rehabilitation where acute illness is concerned.

If those concerned with securing a greater share of society's resources for chronic medical problems try to do so by arguing that these problems are nothing more than a subspecies of the general class of disease, chronic illness and disability will be subject to the same models, standards, evaluative criteria, and professional control as acute illness. The resulting threat to independence and autonomy posed by dependency on the medical system and medical professionals may be a higher price than the chronically ill and disabled ought to be willing to pay.

Time and again newpaper and television broadcasts show how difficult it is for the acutely ill to retain control over their own medical care.[8] Decisions are often made with little or no consultation with competent patients. And when competent patients issue clear directives about the nature and course of their care, be they Jehovah's Witnesses or members of the Hemlock Society, physicians and hospital administrators sometimes pay little attention. All too often the only way of retaining autonomy over health care decisions concerning one's own body is to threaten a lawsuit or media campaign.

A very real danger of extending the medical model to chronic illness is the potential loss of personal freedom and autonomy to professionals. Thus, calls to extend acute care models of medical practice to settings such as nursing homes must be viewed with caution. While turning a nursing home into a hospital or a private home into an intensive care unit may improve the quality of care for the elderly who reside in it, personal autonomy may yield to the kind of professional authority that characterizes the practice of acute care medicine. There is little time for talk in the increasingly impersonal and technological world of acute care medicine.[9]

Are We Obligated to Help the Sick?

Americans, despite their aversion to chiselers, malingerers, and sluggards, do acknowledge a moral obligation to help those who cannot help themselves. Those with acute illnesses have been able to secure a share of public funds obtained by compulsory taxation primarily on the ethical ground that each citizen has an obligation to help meet the health needs of others who are unable to meet their own needs.

The citizens of the United States like to believe that those with heart attacks or broken bones will not be left to fend for themselves even if they lack the means to pay for treatment. Our public philosophy seems to be that those who become acutely ill or who suffer acute injuries are entitled to receive government assistance as long as they can demonstrate clear-cut need. The existence of a need is seen as necessary to create an obligation on the part of society.

Recent interest in making transplants available without regard to the ability of the recipient to pay and in providing catastrophic health insurance coverage reflects precisely this degree of perceived moral obligation on the part of the public. In health care, unlike other areas of life, a need for life-saving medical treatment is held by most citizens to be a sufficient moral ground for requiring others to help pay for its provision, assuming that the needy cannot afford to pay out of their own pockets.

Why should this be so? Why is it that in a society that tolerates enormous differences in access to housing, education, and employment opportunities, health needs occupy a position of special moral standing?

To understand why health care needs elicit a degree of compassion that other needs do not, it is necessary to consider the moral foundations of beneficence in American society. Nearly every moral theory that has any currency in our society posits a duty of beneficence, a duty to aid when the following conditions are met:[10]

1. A need is obvious, serious, and life-threatening.

2. Assistance rendered must stand some chance of meeting or alleviating the need.

3. Those requiring assistance from others must not have any reasonable alternative sources of aid.

4. Providing assistance must not create undue burdens on or risks to those giving the help.

These conditions say nothing about the liability or culpability of those who are in need. At least when lives hang in the balance, our society has remained relatively indifferent to the cause of a person's need in determining a general obligation of beneficence. People who do not wear seat belts or whose drinking leads to the need for a liver transplant may receive aid from publicly funded sources if the conditions outlined above are met. We do not, at least in theory, make allocation decisions based on the worthiness of patients or their social status.[11]

If the major moral outlooks current in our society, both religious and secular, countenance at least a minimal duty of beneficence—an obligation to help others or to meet the needs of others when the conditions outlined above are met—then it is easy to see why life-threatening medical needs have generated so much concern in American health policy. People who have heart attacks or sudden renal failure have clear-cut, life-threatening needs and are not in a position to help themselves. Since in most cases it does not cost very much to pay for the services required to help each individual and since health care professionals know how to treat heart or kidney failure, it would seem that we have a duty to provide resources or to tolerate a degree of taxation sufficient to enable those who cannot pay for the requisite services to have access to them.

But clarifying the moral underpinnings of this obligation of beneficence reveals why those with chronic medical problems may continue to find it difficult to tap into the same vein of moral concern—even in a society as enamored of independence and personal autonomy as the United States. Chronic conditions and disability do not tap the same reservoir of beneficence as acute illness and injury.

Chronic conditions, although they can be severely limiting and can cause serious dysfunction, often lack the obvious need for assistance associated with acute illness. Those in chronic pain with hypertension, diabetes, or arthritis may not be visibly in need of help. Those with disabling injuries or suffering the aftereffects of a mild stroke, while surely in need of assistance, are nevertheless still able to perform many of the activities of day-to-day living.

Chronic conditions and disability not only permit disagreement and uncertainty about a person's level of need, but also have not been demonstrated to be as responsive to treatments as most acute medical problems.

In general, physicians and nurses know how to help those with acute medical problems. Although organ transplants sometimes fail and not every heart attack victim can be saved, the vast array of everyday health problems admit of a course of treatment that is both routine and likely to work.

It is generally not clear, however, and it is far from scientifically proved what kinds of assistance would help those with chronic conditions to gain relief. Whether it be low back pain or rehabilitation after a massive stroke, the efficacy of standard treatments for chronic conditions is not well established.

If more were known about the effectiveness of attempts to re-habilitate persons with spinal cord injuries or coping with chronic pain, perhaps more money would be made available to ensure that persons with these conditions had access to care. But with so little known about whether medical intervention does any good in such cases, it is hard to command a greater share of public resources when so many other claims are being made on them for acute and emer-gency medical services and for other types of social goods (education, defence, public works, and so on).

Matters are made worse by the emphasis our society places on autonomy and free choice. One way to view curing is to see it as restoring a person to a state of autonomy and free choice, unimpaired by illness or disease.[12] But the chronically ill and disabled often are left in permanent states of dependency by their conditions—not an especially popular status in our culture.

The obligation to help the chronically ill and disabled is also weakened by the belief that, whereas only physicians and trained medical personnel can help the acutely ill, many other people—spouses, children, relatives, friends, members of religious and frater-nal organizations—are capable of providing the kind of aid that is in fact most useful for those with chronic medical problems. No one believes that a husband has a special duty to relieve a case of bacterial meningitis that his wife might contract. But many people believe that it is his duty to provide for her should she become blind, wheelchair bound, demented, arthritic, or diabetic. The possibility of family assistance undercuts the moral pressure felt by others to provide for those with chronic medical needs.

Finally, the provision of aid to those with acute illness and injury seems not to entail undue risks or burdens (or at least did not seem to do so until health care costs began escalating rapidly). But chronic conditions demand aid that is burdensome, both financially and in the ways it affects the lives of those giving it. Society views it very differently when a person is asking for help to pay for having a gall bladder removed than when that person requests assistance for spina bifida, Alzheimer's disease, or cystic fibrosis. The needs are great in all cases, but the burden of providing help seems much more onerous and, to put the point baldly, endless in the case of chronic condi-tions.[13]

One final reason for the moral asymmetry between the provision of public funds for acute and chronic medical problems is confusion about whether chronic medical problems or disabilities really are diseases. Uncertainty about the categorization of chronic medical problems condemns those with such impairments and disorders to a kind of conceptual limbo, in which lines of responsibility among those with disabling conditions, their families, health care professionals, social welfare agencies, and other social institutions are not clearly drawn.

Chronic Illness, Disability, and the Medical Model

The dominant philosophical outlook on chronic illness in the United States is that it does not require any special ethical status. Although we are willing to acknowledge the possibility that mental illness differs in important and significant respects from physical illness as a category or type of disease, there is little inclination to consider chronic diseases as constituting a significantly different class from acute conditions.

There are many articles about the limits of the medical model in understanding and treating mental illness, but there are no analogous discussions where chronic disease is concerned. With the possible exception of mental disorders, modern medicine views disease as a single category or, in more philosophical terms, as a natural "kind," with acute and chronic disease just variants on a single theme.

But is this classification valid? Should chronic disease and disability be lumped together with acute illnesses and injuries? Or are there differences significant enough to place them in two separate categories of disease? And if so, do they require different methods of care and different responses from those responsible for creating health policies?

What Is the Medical Model? In the medical model the goal of health care is to cure disease.[14] Disease is defined as any dysfunction of an organ, organ system, or structure,[15] and health is understood as the absence of disease. Those who subscribe to these definitions see little need to make value judgments about whether or not a person is sick; one merely measures the appropriate physiological variables, and the answer is obvious to anyone with the proper training. The medical model presumes that all diseases have quantifiable physiological causes with definite onsets and, if left untreated, predictable outcomes.

Some may protest that this description of the medical model is a straw man, that health care providers know better than to treat patients simply as vessels containing dysfunctional kidneys, bladders, or thyroids. But despite recent efforts to broaden the goals of medical care beyond the narrow aim of restoring normal function, for many kinds of hospital-based medical care this account is accurate.[16] It is certainly a model that dominates many textbooks of surgery, immunology, pathology, infectious disease, and, increasingly, psychiatry.

The Sick Role. One of the most important contributions made by those studying the sociology of medicine has been to show how different the perception of illness by patients and society is from that of professionals within the medical system. Perhaps the best known exposition of the cultural and social dimensions of disease is Talcott Parsons's definition of what he termed the "sick role."[17]

Parsons noted that health and disease have a special status in American society. He observed that in our achievement-oriented society health is given an especially high priority because it is a prerequisite for being able to work, which is a critical capacity in a competitive free-market society.

The social construction of disease, according to Parsons and those who have extended his analyses, is a far cry from the professional understanding of disease as defined by the medical model.[18] Our ordinary understanding of disease—what Parsons termed the sick role, or what might usefully be termed the illness model—is based on four conditions that cause us to recognize someone as ill: a person is incapable of curing himself; is exempt from usual roles and duties; wants to get better; and wants to seek help from experts and to receive treatment.

Disease, Chronic Illness, and Disability—A Poor Fit. What is interesting about the analysis of disease in the medical model and the more expansive analysis in the illness model is that chronic illness and disability do not fit well into either model. Chronic illness and disability are remarkable for the fact that they often lack a clear-cut physiological cause, onset, or outcome. The disabled and the chronically ill cannot have function restored. Part of the very definition of a chronic condition is that it is incurable. Moreover, many of the problems of the chronically ill have as much to do with sociology and politics as with physiology.

Those with chronic conditions obviously would like medicine to cure or alleviate their disabilities. But in lieu of cures, access to buildings, jobs, housing, and education are of greater concern than what neurology, rehabilitation medicine, or psychiatry has to offer.

Even at the social level, though, the chronically ill and disabled are in trouble even under the illness model. To some extent health care professionals in particular and society in general hold the chronically ill responsible for their own cures.

Motivation and compliance are the virtues expected of the chronically ill and disabled in health care settings. Patients seen to have "motivational problems" risk fast abandonment by their health care professionals. Society has equally high expectations, at least to the extent to which the media celebrate those who have stopped "whining" about their ailments and gotten on with their lives.

The chronically ill and disabled, while exempt from some social roles and duties, are often capable of doing what everyone else does—if society will let them. They face a peculiar Catch-22 dilemma, though: they want to carry out the roles and duties that they are capable of, but they must depend on society's recognition that they cannot and should not be expected to carry out *all* the usual roles.

As noted earlier, a key ethical requirement for feeling a duty of beneficence to another is that the recipient be truly in need of help. Yet a critical precondition for receiving respect from others in our society is that a person not be perceived as dependent, needy, or receiving aid. The acutely ill can face this dilemma with the knowledge that their state is temporary. The disabled and the chronically ill have a much harder time of it, since their needs are seemingly endless.

The chronically ill and disabled often encounter medical problems that require professional help. But, like those who require only brief, episodic interactions with the world of medicine to cope with acute or emergency medical problems, they do not want to spend their entire lives dependent on health care institutions and professionals. Thus, they do and yet do not want to seek out medical expertise, another tension that tends to delegitimate the authenticity of their needs and claims.

On strictly medical grounds, chronic illness and disability do not fit the model of disease that prevails within our medical system.[19] Nevertheless, there are many reasons for those who are chronically ill and disabled to conform to the requirements of that model, both to gain access to the medical system and to gain legitimacy for their conditions in a society disinclined to be tolerant of anyone who will not pull his own economic weight.

The wisdom of securing resources or the sympathy of the public by squeezing chronic illness and disability into the medical model, however, is disputable, as some health policy commentators have cogently observed.[20] The goals of the chronically ill and the disabled are not necessarily those of the acute care patient. If chronic illness and disability are not readily subsumed under the standard definition of disease and illness, meeting the needs of the chronically ill and disabled may require a redefinition of their problems as well as a reassessment of the kinds of services that can best meet their needs.

Reclassifying Chronic Illness and Disease

To a great extent, recent policy debates about chronic illness focus on whether it is worthwhile for society to invest resources in medical care that results in large numbers of persons living longer but being sicker.[21] As the pressure to contain health care costs escalates, policy options are framed as requiring a choice between paying for acute medical care needs of the many and providing exotic care for the unusual medical care needs of the few.[22] The needs of children, the mentally ill, the elderly, the disabled, the dying, and the chronically ill are seen as competing against one another for a finite and diminishing pool of resources.

Is it necessary, however, to see health policy as constrained by the need to make hard choices among the competing claims of those with various types of disorders and diseases? Is it true that what constitutes optimal care for one group will necessarily be the same for others?

As we have already seen, there are significant differences between the definitions of acute and chronic diseases. These differences significantly weaken attempts to fit chronic illness under the rubric of acute disease or to draw upon the kinds of arguments for beneficence that have been persuasive in pushing our society to meet the acute and emergency medical needs of its poor and elderly.

The solution to helping those with chronic diseases and disabilities may not require government officials and physicians to perform health care triage. Rather, the prospects of governmental fiscal insolvency occasioned by the provision of public funds for chronic illness and disability might be lessened if they could be removed from the domain of the medical model of disease and placed in a separate category. Such a redefinition might contribute to a more precise understanding of both chronic illness and disability while appealing to the beneficent impulses of the American public to help those who cannot meet their own needs, either for want of economic means or for lack of willing helpers.

The Chronically Ill and Disabled Are Not Diseased

The solution to the public policy dilemma of how to afford the costs associated with chronic illness and disability is very much a function of the classification or conceptualization of these conditions. We have seen that chronic illness and disability do not meet the requirements of the traditional medical model of disease. Surprisingly, they do not conform to the criteria of a more inclusive illness model either. And perhaps most surprisingly, they do not meet the requirements for eliciting a duty of beneficence on the part of others as this obligation is understood under most theories of ethics.

Two strategies might be chosen in light of these findings. One approach would be to broaden either the standard medical model of disease or the illness model to incorporate chronic illness and disability. In doing so, it may be possible to appeal to the same principle of beneficence that has proved so effective in securing resources for those with acute or catastrophic diseases.

The other strategy would be simply to admit that chronic conditions and disability, while often having their roots in disease or illness, are conceptually distinct from these categories. Although those who are disabled or chronically ill often endure medical crises just as other members of society do, it may be conceptually confusing—and may deprive them of their autonomy—to lump them under a medical or illness model of disease.

Numerous advocacy groups for the disabled and the chronically ill have objected to the notion that those with chronic impairments or disabilities ought to be viewed as permanently sick. Such a classification, while commanding great moral force for securing resources from the health care system under the principle of beneficence, comes at a high price. It means that the chronically ill and disabled will be seen by both health care professionals and society as permanent patients meriting assistance, but also meriting paternalistic charitable aid. In a society that treasures independence and autonomy, assuming the role of permanent patient is not likely to ensure the dignity and equality of those in constant need of medical treatment.

"Demedicalizing" Chronic Illness and Disability

In listening to what those with disabilities or chronic impairments say they want, it becomes plain that we need to abandon the attempt to squeeze them into the framework of disease or illness or to make them the recipients of societal beneficence by expanding their access to models of care inspired by acute care medicine. Those with impairments or disabilities that are not immediately life-threatening do not want constant access to medical care and the ministrations of health care professionals; they want to be given the same opportunities other Americans enjoy to maximize their abilities and capacities.

The disabled seek equality of opportunity with respect to housing, education, employment, and recreation. They wish to be seen as
ordinary citizens who may require social interventions or accommodations to allow them to participate as fully as possible in the
ordinary activities of daily life. Consequently, efforts to expand the
medical system to absorb more of the chronically ill and disabled,
while well motivated, are misguided. Of course, the medical needs of
the chronically ill and disabled ought to be met, but on the same
moral grounds that our society recognizes as appropriate for guaran-
teeing access to health care for any citizen, disabled, impaired, or not.

To argue that we need more medical specialists in chronic illness
or disability, more hospitals and long-term care facilities for the
chronically ill and disabled, and a greater emphasis on the provision
of medical therapies for the disabled is to miss the point. What many
of those with chronic illnesses or disabilities need is equal opportunity, not beneficence or charity. The acutely ill or those facing catastrophic health care emergencies require our beneficence and charity,
but those with chronic illness or disabilities who are not facing an
acute medical crisis deserve something radically different—the right
to equality of opportunity.

The key to sound public policy with respect to chronic illness and
disability is not the creation of more teaching nursing homes in
academic medical centers or a greater emphasis on chronic illness in
our schools of nursing or medicine. Medical professionals need to
understand the nature of acute illness in a person with impairments
or disabilities to the extent that such illness is more likely or different
when disabilities are present. But those with chronic illness or impairments need from society less emphasis on the medical aspects of
chronic disease and more emphasis on the social adjustments necessary to assist them in becoming full participants in society.

In other words, the disabled and chronically ill have a right to
expect the "demedicalization" of chronic disease in favor of the provision of social services, educational programs, the removal of architectural barriers, and vocational training. We need social policies aimed
at restoring and enhancing the autonomy of persons whose impairments or disorders cannot be cured.

The moral foundation for access to such services is different from
that for claiming access to medical services that are beyond a person's
financial means. Those with disabilities or chronic impairments can
lay claim to requisite social services for themselves or those with
whom they live on the grounds that, while they may be no more
entitled to equality of outcome than any other citizen, they are entitled to equality of opportunity. Those with non-life-threatening

chronic impairments cannot be cured, but they can require social policies that maximize their opportunities for choice and freedom.

To say that those with chronic illnesses or impairments do not require access to health care is not to say that they need little or no contact with physicians, nurses, and other health care providers. Obviously, many aspects of chronic illness or disability are amenable to some forms of medical intervention, either for the palliation of symptoms or because those with chronic conditions may be more vulnerable to acute or emergency medical problems than other members of society are.

To say that the social or public policy response to chronic illness is better formulated under the rubric of opportunity than of beneficence is to say that access to health care should not be the major preoccupation of public policy. This is not because it would be expensive to attempt to help those with chronic impairments or disorders in this way, although in fact it would be. It is because treating chronic illness and disability strictly as medical problems requiring medical responses "disenfranchises" a large segment of society by making them permanent objects of social beneficence, a status that few if any members of our society would wish to occupy.

If the chronically ill and disabled can be weaned from the medical system, they may be able to reach their full potential at less cost. Moreover, every individual's enjoyment of autonomy and independence may be enriched.

Chronic illness and disability have a remarkable power. Those who endure a disability must think long and hard about the nature of their own identity and about what it is that they want to be and become. The onset of a chronic illness or disabling condition may actually enhance autonomy by forcing direct decisions about goals, personal plans, values, and life-style choices, which are all too often pushed aside by the able-bodied or healthy as too frightening.

Perhaps it is easier to fit chronic illness and disability into a medical or illness model because doing so avoids the challenge that impairment and disability pose to our sense of personal identity and responsibility. The impaired and the disabled become persons worthy of charity, not of choices.

Chronic illness and disability remind us all not only of our technological or scientific limits but also of how difficult it is to be truly independent or autonomous. While we pay much lip service to these lofty notions in our political rhetoric, the prospect of confronting choices about who we are and who we really want to be is simply too terrifying for many of us. Disability is a reminder that to be truly autonomous one must be willing to reflect consciously on one's identity and aspirations. If that is so, the appropriate public policy response is not to figure out how our society can afford to pay for access to medical technology or health care professionals for those with chronic illness or disability. Rather, it is to confront, openly and honestly, the challenge of creating social policies that are necessary to enhance the opportunities of those who lack certain abilities or capacities. Reflection on the ways our society can maximize opportunities for those with impairments and permanent disabilities will inevitably enhance the freedom and autonomy of everyone, disabled or not.

Notes

1. James F. Fries, "Aging, Natural Death, and the Compression of Morbidity," *New England Journal of Medicine*, vol. 303 (1980), pp. 130–35; E. Schneider and J. Brody, "Aging, Natural Death, and the Compression of Morbidity: Another View," *New England Journal of Medicine*, vol. 309, no. 14 (1983), pp. 854–56; and Lois Verbrugge, "Longer Life but Worsening Health?" *Milbank Memorial Fund Quarterly*, vol. 62, no. 3 (1984), pp. 475–519.

2. Henry Aaron and William Schwartz, *The Painful Prescription* (Washington, D.C.: Brookings Institution, 1984); Jerry Avorn, "Benefit and Cost Analysis in Geriatric Care," *New England Journal of Medicine*, vol. 310 (1984), pp. 1294–1301; Joseph Califano, *America's Health Care Revolution* (New York: Random House, 1986); Roger W. Evans, "Healthcare Technology and Resource Allocation," *Journal of the American Medical Association*, vol. 249, no. 15 (1983), pp. 2047–53; Richard D. Lamm, *Megatraumas* (New York: Houghton Mifflin, 1985); and Richard D. Lamm, "We Can't Afford the Health Plan," *New York Times*, February 19, 1984, p. A31.

3. Irving Lewis and Cecil Sheps, *The Sick Citadel* (Boston: Oelgeschlager, Gunn and Hain, 1983); and Paul Starr, *The Social Transformation of American Medicine* (New York: Basic Books, 1983).

4. Gerben DeJong and R. Lifchez, "Physical Disability and Public Policy," *Scientific American*, vol. 248, no. 6 (1983), pp. 40–49.

5. Norman Daniels, *Just Health Care* (New York: Cambridge University Press, 1985).

6. Lamm, *Megatraumas*; and Lamm, "We Can't Afford the Health Plan."

7. Arthur Caplan, "Kidneys, Ethics, and Politics," *Journal of Health Politics, Policy, and Law*, vol. 6, no. 3 (1981), pp. 488–503.

8. George Annas, "Transferring the Ethical Hot Potato," *Hastings Center Report*, vol. 17, no. 1 (1987), pp. 20–21.

9. Jay Katz, *The Silent World of Doctor and Patient* (New York: Free Press, 1986).

10. Tom Beauchamp and James Childress, *Principles of Biomedical Ethics* (New York: Oxford University Press, 1979).

11. Arthur Caplan, "Equity in the Selection of Recipients for Cardiac Transplants," *Circulation*, vol. 75, no. 1 (1987), pp. 10–20.

12. Eric Cassell, *The Healer's Art* (Cambridge, Mass.: MIT Press, 1985).

13. C. Weiner et al., "What Price Chronic Illness?" *Society*, vol. 19, no. 2 (1982), pp. 22–30.

14. Arthur Caplan, "The Concepts of Health and Disease," in R. Veatch, ed., *Medical Ethics* (forthcoming).

15. Christopher Boorse, "On the Distinction between Disease and Illness," in Arthur Caplan et al., eds., *Concepts of Health and Disease* (Reading, Mass.: Addison-Wesley, 1981), pp. 545–60.

16. George Engel, "The Need for a New Medical Model," in Caplan et al., *Concepts of Health and Disease*, pp. 589–608.

17. Talcott Parsons, "Definitions of Health and Illness in the Light of American Values and Social Structures," in Caplan et al., *Concepts of Health and Disease*, pp. 57–82.

18. David Mechanic, "Illness Behavior, Social Adaptation, and the Management of Illness," *Journal of Nervous and Mental Disease*, vol. 165, no. 2 (1977), pp. 79–87.

19. Gerben DeJong, "Medical Models and Ethical Systems," forthcoming.

20. Muriel Gillick, "Is the Care of the Chronically Ill a Medical Prerogative?" *New England Journal of Medicine*, vol. 310, no. 3 (1984), pp. 190–93; and Anne Somers, "Long-Term Care for the Elderly and Disabled—A New Health Priority," *New England Journal of Medicine*, vol. 307, no. 4 (1982), pp. 221–26.

21. Verbrugge, "Longer Life but Worsening Health?"; and Bruce Vladek and J. Firman, "The Aging of the Population and Health Services," *Annals of the American Academy of Political and Social Sciences*, vol. 468 (July 1983), pp. 132–48.

22. Aaron and Schwartz, *The Painful Prescription*; Lamm, *Megatraumas*; and Lamm, "We Can't Afford."

5
Policies and Programs Concerning Aging and Disability: Toward a Unifying Agenda

Irving Kenneth Zola

There's no news, only olds.

RUSSELL BAKER

The syndicated columnist Russell Baker once used these words to characterize the bulk of information featured in the daily news media. It is an appropriate caveat for this paper. Much of the information in this paper is neither new nor news. In fact, I hope the readers sense that they have read most of it before. My intention in highlighting the olds, however, is to reinforce empirically and conceptually what many have long thought necessary—a unified agenda in health care policy for those who are aging and those who have disabilities.

The following words, describing the current crisis in care, help set such an agenda:

> The crisis is one both of results and of expenditure. The crisis of expenditure has arisen because the cost of care is outstripping the economic scope available. Unless the structure and working methods of care are changed, there is a grave risk of social retrenchment to the detriment of the disadvantaged groups in society. Secondly, the results of care do not measure up to the demands which one should be entitled to make of it. The visible problems of waiting lists and waiting periods, difficulties of finding one's way in the care system and impersonal, indifferent treatment are accompanied by profounder problems connected with the ideology and the concept[s] . . . characterizing [such] care and with the paramount influence acquired by professionals on the direction and methods of care.[1]

This critical statement was made *not* about care in the United States, but about care in the country generally recognized as having the most enduring and encompassing commitment to the general welfare of its population—Sweden. Although the problems in care will certainly vary from one political and economic system to another, they may nevertheless have certain common qualities, at least in the Western world.

Current Issues in Disability and Care

Five overlapping issues form the substance of this paper. They involve a series of analytically separate but empirically related phenomena: the almost inexorable increase in the prevalence of disabling conditions in our society; the continually changing nature of those conditions; the effect of the processes of "technicalization" and "medicalization" on the care that is being delivered; the implications, difficulties, and possibilities of a shift in care from institutions into the home; and the identification and empowerment of those traditionally perceived as in need of care.

The number of people with conditions that interfere with their full participation in society will inevitably increase. Estimates of the number of people with disabilities in the United States vary enormously, depending on the purpose and source of the data.[2] Frank Bowe, using the 1980 Census of Population and Housing, says there are over 12 million working-age disabled persons (8.5 percent of the working-age population) in this country and 21 million disabled persons overall (8 percent of the total population).[3] The National Center for Health Statistics, using "reported chronic diseases" as a correlate of activity limitation, estimates the number of people with a disability at over 31 million (11.8 percent), while the Office of Technology Assessment, using a combination of methods, uses the figure of 45 million (17 percent).[4] Since most such statistics are based on subsets of the population and too often omit people with mental disabilities, institutionalized populations, and persons over sixty-five and under twenty, David Pfeiffer argues that all these figures are underestimates.[5] Reworking the data, he claims that 30 to 45 percent of the current population either have a disability or are regarded as having one.

Although these figures are large enough in themselves to be of concern, the major issue is whether or not they are likely to continue increasing.[6] Recent declines in various mortality statistics (the total death rate, infant and maternal mortality, condition-specific death rates, increases in life expectancy at birth and at various later ages) and changes in access to and the costs and effectiveness of medical interventions and even of certain behaviors (smoking, diet, exercise) cause

91

many to claim that the health of America is improving. Time series studies of illness and disability, however, provide a different and less optimistic picture.

When Wilson and Drury reviewed the twenty-year trends in fifteen broad categories of chronic illness (1960 to 1981), they found that the prevalence of seven conditions (heart disease, diabetes, hypertension, bronchitis/sinusitis, arthritis/rheumatism, visual impairments, and hearing impairments) had more than doubled.[7] Two conditions had increased in prevalence 50 to 99 percent (asthma/hay fever and impairments of back or spine), five had increased up to 50 percent (peptic ulcer, hernia, paralysis, varicose veins, and hemorrhoids); and only one condition (impairments of lower extremities) had become less prevalent. The so-called graying of the population did not explain the increases, since a similar pattern was observed for persons forty-five to sixty-four. For this latter group—the core of the working population—these figures translated directly into limitations on activity, more than doubling (from 4.4 percent o 10.8 percent) the number of males who claimed they were unable to work because of some illness or disability.

Looking at the two subsets—the young and the old, whom Pfeiffer considered to be understudied and underrepresented—is equally instructive. All census data affirm that the fastest growing segment of the U.S. population is made up of those over the age of sixty-five. In 1880 their number was less than 2 million (3 percent of the total population), but by 1980 it was 25 million (11.3 percent). By the year 2030 an estimated one in four or five citizens is likely to be over sixty-five. Put another way, throughout most of history only one in ten people lived past sixty-five; now nearly 80 percent do.

This traditional use of sixty-five as a benchmark is deceptive, for the most phenomenal growth will be in the even older age groups. In the decade 1980 to 1990, the sixty-five to seventy-four age group is expected to increase about 14 percent while the seventy-five to eighty-four group will grow 27 percent and the eighty-five and older group about 20 percent. By the year 2000 the sixty-five to seventy-four group may decline slightly, the seventy-five to eighty-four group rise 16 percent, and the eighty-five and older group grow 29 percent.[8] Patrice Hirsch Feinstein, Marian Gornick, and Jay N. Greenberg suggest the service implications of these figures by noting that 3 percent of persons sixty-five to sixty-nine need assistance with personal care but by eighty-five 33 percent do.[9]

The data on children are equally significant, for the absolute numbers in this age group (under seventeen) are not expected to increase. The National Health Interview Survey indicates that the prevalence of activity-limiting chronic conditions among children doubled between 1960 and 1981, from 1.8 percent to 3.8 percent, with the greatest increase in the past decade.[10] While major advances are being made in keeping many lower-weight newborns alive and many of these children survive with disabilities, the increase may well be due to shifting perceptions of parents, educators, and physicians. Health care professionals often refer to this as "the new morbidity," a trend away from the concern of pediatric practice with traditional medical illness toward greater interest in psychosocial issues such as behavioral adjustments and learning difficulties.[11] (Later in this paper this process is referred to as medicalization.)

Although some have argued that the new concern results in part from the increased supply of pediatricians needing new territories in which to practice, it has been reinforced by the growing attention of other health professionals, educators, and the general public to learning and other educational difficulties. Implementation of the Education for all Handicapped Children Act of 1975 (P.L. 94-142) and renewed efforts at "mainstreaming" disabled children sharpened the focus on them. In fact, while census data from 1970 to 1980 show little change in the number of children institutionalized for physical disabilities, the number institutionalized for mental disabilities declined. Hence, it appears that the recent increase in the prevalence of learning disabilities among noninstitutionalized children may be explained by increased detection efforts and heightened awareness of educational problems, as well as by efforts to deinstitutionalize and provide mainstream education for mentally disabled children.[12] It is also clear that changing educational concerns are making "learning problems" the fastest growing disability on college campuses.[13] What new learning disabilities we will discover as computer literacy becomes a *sine qua non* for success in contemporary society is anybody's guess.

Nearly thirty years ago, René Dubos made the following observation:

> Organized species such as ants have established a satisfactory equilibrium and suffer no great waves of diseases or changes in their social structure. But man is essentially dynamic, his way of life constantly in flux from century to century. He experiments with synthetic products and changes his diet; he builds cities that breed rats and infestation; he builds automobiles and factories which pollute the air; and he constructs radioactive bombs. As life becomes more comfortable and technology more complicated, new

factors introduce new dangers; the ingredients for Utopia are the agents of new disease.[14]

Thus, whether measured by the prevalence of certain chronic conditions, by limitations in activity, by the aging of the population, or by the awareness of parents and professionals and the demands and structure of society, the number of people with conditions interfering with their full social participation is steadily increasing.

Those with "disabling" conditions and differences will live longer, and the nature of their disabilities will change. For years infant mortality has steadily decreased, in large part because of improvements in standards of living and prenatal care. Recently those improvements have been supplemented by advances in the new specialization of neonatology.[15] Increasing numbers of low-birth-weight and other infants are surviving into childhood and beyond with manifest chronic impairments. With advances in medical therapeutics, many children who would have died (such as those suffering from leukemia, spina bifida, or cystic fibrosis) are now surviving into adulthood. Diagnostic advances, as well as some life-extending technologies, allow many young people to survive with so-called terminal illnesses. The new medical specialty—thanatology—and social concern with the process of dying reflect the existence of new life-extending technologies.[16]

With the advent of other therapeutic and preventive advances, it is predicted that middle-age fitness will probably improve. According to Fries and others, however, the improvement will not eliminate disease and disability but rather will produce a "compression of morbidity" toward the end of the life span.[17] The previous section noted that professional and societal changes have led to attention to the "new" problems of the young and newborn; the same may occur for the elderly. Jan Blanpain argues that as society grows older medical authorities will devote greater attention to quality-of-life issues and to extending the active, rather than the purely biological, life span, and thus

> interventions aiming at pure symptomatic treatment of the discomforts caused by intractable pathology—in order to restore or safeguard "effective" functioning of individuals and to increase the active lifespan—become legitimate competitors in the allocation of scarce resources.[18]

Moreover, in an aging population more people will experience natural decreases in mobility, visual acuity, and hearing as well as musculoskeletal, cardiovascular, and cerebrovascular changes, the implications of which are only beginning to be appreciated.

Still another unappreciated aspect of most chronic conditions is that, though permanent, they are not necessarily static. While we do, of course, recognize that some diseases are progressive, we are less inclined to see that there is no one-time, overall adaptation or adjustment to the condition, no set treatment, and—most important—no design requirement for an individual's working and living situations. Even for a recognized progressive and episodic disorder such as multiple sclerosis, only recently has attention been given to the continuing nature of adaptations.[19] The same is also true for those with end-stage renal disease.[20] With the survival into adulthood of people with diseases that once were usually fatal come changes and complications. Problems of circulation and vision for people with diabetes, for example, may be due to the disease itself, to the aging process, or even to the life-sustaining treatment.[21] Ivan Illich has drawn attention to the iatrogenic costs of many medical interventions—costs that may show up only after many years, as one ages, or in subsequent generations (a rare vaginal cancer in children of mothers who took the drug DES to prevent miscarriage is one example).[22]

Perhaps the most telling example of a new manifestation of an old disease is the current concern over the so-called post-polio syndrome. To most of the public, to clinicians, and certainly to its bearers, poliomyelitis has been considered a stable chronic illness. Following its acute onset and a period of rehabilitation, most people reached a plateau and expected to stay there. For the majority this may still be true, but for at least a quarter of us it is not. According to the latest reports, some twenty to forty years after the original onset, large numbers of people are experiencing new problems.[23] The most common are fatigue, weakness in muscles previously affected and unaffected, muscle and joint pain, breathing difficulties, and intolerance to cold. Whether these new problems are the mere concomitants of aging, the reemergence of a still lingering virus, a long-term effect of the early damage or even of the early rehabilitation programs, or something else is still at issue. Whatever the etiology of this phenomenon, there will probably be many more new manifestations of old diseases and disabilities as people survive decades beyond the acute onset of their conditions. Thus, the dichotomy between those people with a progressive condition and those with a static one may well be, generally speaking, much more narrow and may even be a more continuous phenomenon.

In other instances, it is not so much the underlying condition that changes as the situation in which it occurs. In studying an older population, May Clarke found that between 55 and 90 percent (respondent report versus chiropodist examination) of her sample of

1,100 adults had something the matter with their feet.[24] The conditions ranged from corns to skin infections, from ingrown toenails to hammertoes. Only 17 percent of these problems had ever been treated, and though clinically not "serious," they were often painful and inconvenient and, for the older population, "functionally crippling," preventing them from traveling or walking any considerable distance and eventually resulting in even greater isolation.

All of these findings are further complicated by the tabulation methods and thus inadvertently distort somewhat the portrayal of the prevalence of impairments, diseases, and chronic conditions.[25] Every disease rate is computed independently, and the rates presented are per thousand or larger population group. None of these rates by itself is particularly high, and since cross-codings or cross-tabulations are made only for select populations (for example, to demonstrate the existence of multiproblem families), there is never a complete or even necessarily an accurate picture.

The strength of this view of the "singularity of disease" was conveyed to me by an investigator who had received a grant to study the coping reactions of people to a first myocardial infarct. He was petitioning a review panel for an extension because he was having difficulty getting a "pure" sample; that is, he discovered that a myocardial infarct was not the only major problem of his respondents. Most of those on the panel sympathized with his dilemma, and he was allowed to spend the next several months designing a way of "controlling" this fact out of existence. To me, he was doing more. He was controlling reality. For by trying to ignore the fact that a myocardial infarct was just one of many medical and other problems with which his patients had to cope, he was altering their reality and compromising the utility of his findings. Similarly, while there is some clinical recognition that most people with a disease are likely to have more than one (particularly as they age), the trend toward specialization of both medical and social services belies this simple yet important fact.

Implicit in all that I have written is the notion that disabling conditions are the result not merely of some physical or mental impairment but rather of the fit of such impairments with the social, attitudinal, architectural, and even political environment. In recent years a movement has grown around this thesis, and critics have begun to delineate its implications for social policy.[26] Simply put, some physical differences become important only in certain social environments (reading and writing difficulties in a literate environment, mobility impairments in a sports-oriented society) or at certain times of life (sexual and reproductive issues are less important for the very young and the very old, and some are important for only one sex). The life-cycle theorists are quite aware of this and postulate different issues we must contend with and the resulting disablements if we do not do so.[27] Yet many of these theories and the resulting social policies are locked into a grid where the "final" stage of life begins around age sixty-five. This might have been at least logical when the general life span was much shorter; then each stage took about ten years. But what does it imply when the "last" stage continues far beyond a decade, with some estimating it could reach well over a hundred. Surely neither society in general nor the individuals involved will tolerate one stage of life that covers half of the life span. My sense is that later life is an uncharted map that will inevitably bring new challenges requiring different capacities and evaluations, but also involving new diseases and disabilities.

Thus, while today's chronic conditions may be around for longer periods of time, their quality, scope, and dimensions will not be permanent.

The process of technicalization can lead to the objectification of care and attitudes of the people who give and receive care. The United States seems to be a nation built on the premise that, with great effort and the right technique, there is no mountain that cannot be climbed and no force of nature that cannot be harnessed. This philosophy has put us in the forefront of applied science. Where medicine was concerned, this took form in the age of magic bullets that cured and prevented a large number of infectious diseases. The diseases of the late twentieth century do not seem to yield to such once-and-for-all solutions. Medical miracles continue to occur, but more take the form of life-extending technologies.[28] In recent decades these have included organ transplants, bionic and genetic engineering, and enhanced pharmacopeia.

Such high-technology development, however, not only does not follow any "natural" progression but also is subject to many extra-medical influences (and scarcely any consumer input).[29] To cite but two recent examples, the development of DES and the dissemination of the CAT scanner were influenced by the conflictive and cooperative relationships and interests of medical practitioners, scientific researchers, federal regulatory agencies, and the pharmaceutical and computer industries.[30] With so many interests involved, it is easy to understand that, once begun and even with recurring and unanswered questions of efficacy and safety, the processes were difficult, if not impossible, to discontinue.

These personal and societal investments in technologies have inevitable costs. The publicity generated by artificial heart transplants and electrical stimulation for spinal cord injuries cannot help but divert economic and psychological resources. The glamour of such high-tech solutions detracts from the importance of necessary improvements in such low-technology aids as wheelchairs and crutches and even hampers the development of ones necessary to daily existence.[31] Too often forgotten, also, is the very long lead time between the development of these devices or procedures and their eventual wider and cheaper dissemination. Thus, it is unlikely that any of the techniques currently in their earliest phase of development will ever be of use in the lives of the majority of those who currently have major heart conditions or spinal cord injuries. In short, such people need to adapt to their limitations, to enhance their functional capacities, and to make accommodations to their social and physical environment.[32]

The conquering aspect of technology has a counterpart in the passivity of the recipients of care. Early models of medical care went so far as to claim that passivity was a necessary condition of good care.[33] Eventually this became a self-fulfilling prophecy, with patients as well as professionals believing that experts had to take complete responsibility for solving problems because helpless patients lacked the capacity and the will to handle and solve their own problems. Care based on this approach raises exaggerated expectations (a seedbed for malpractice suits) and undermines the capacity of individuals to draw on their own resources when they most need them—when faced with frustrating, long-term, often intractable problems. It is thus no great surprise that people who learn to normalize and routinize their situations do far better, for example, in dealing with many of the problems of hemodialysis in end-stage renal disease.[34]

Faith in the technological cure encourages belief in the fallacy that all problems have a technical solution and creates a bias in favor of short-term gains over long-term consequences. It also creates a preference for solving problems that can be measured and described in objective terms over those with more social and psychological dimensions.

Independence, the traditional hallmark of success in rehabilitation, is a good example. It has often been measured by functional performance (self-care, toileting, dressing, often called "activities in daily living") and its philosophy embedded in the instruction "to use it or lose it" and to push oneself to the limits of one's physical capacity. But living by this measure of independence means engaging in activities only when they can be performed under one's own steam. This may be a definition of "mainstreaming," but it is not necessarily one of "independence." Many people with hand-propelled wheelchairs may limit their social activities to those that can be conducted in a range of a few hundred yards, while with an electronic chair their mobility can be measured in miles. The same rationale applies to doing certain tasks by oneself, or with help, or not at all. The independent living movement crystallizes this issue very well.[35] Its very philosophy proclaims a new notion of independence, measured not by the mundane physical tasks one can do but by the personal and economic decisions one can make—not by the quantity of tasks one can perform without assistance but by the quality of life one can live with help.

There are other even more subtle ways in which the use of technology has gone and is going too far—putting an individual's very integrity at stake. There is very little understanding of what happens when bodily parts and functions are replaced by equipment; it is not an unmixed blessing. It has been found in recipients of transplants and skin grafts that the physiological body rejects parts it feels are alien. So, too, the psychosocial person rejects parts he or she feels are alien and often experiences profound feelings of distrust, anger, depression, and even suicide. Thus, for someone who must put on braces or strap on prosthetic limbs as part of his daily routine, the adjustment may become more serious, if not psychosis-producing, as people become *internally* attached to and thus dependent on machines, such as pacemakers or kidney dialysis machines.

The overtechnicalization of care, such as in the invention of robots or the training of chimpanzees to serve, dress, and feed quadraplegics, may create a similar problem. Part of the appeal of machines and animals is the intimacy that people may perceive is easier to share with them. But there may be a long-term loss from this short-term gain. I did not accidentally use the term "care" when introducing this thought. According to Webster's dictionary, care involves painstaking or watchful attention, regard coming from desire or esteem, and a person that is an object of attention, anxiety, or solicitude.

The point is simple—that giving medical care or personal care is not merely a technical task. On the contrary, it is quite personal. Thus to objectify this care by replacing a human being with a machine or an animal can only lead to the further objectification of the individual receiving care. Moreover, when the technical side of care is so prominent that it becomes the same as care itself, a situation ripe for ethical tragedy is created. In the fall of 1981, three Boston physicians were convicted of rape. While out on appeal, one of the doctors got a job in another state. He was able to do so on the basis of the recommendations of other physicians, including superiors, who later claimed that other matters (the rapes he had committed) did not affect his practice of good technical medicine.[36]

Of course, much traditional care giving has also produced problems. Patronizing attitudes by physicians, for example, are not a good thing. But as bad as such behavior is, at least it is human, reinforcing the humanness of the individuals involved. Being handled by a machine or an animal when one was used to being handled by a person can only cause a feeling of "invalidation."

Finally, the continuing technical focus (despite lip service to the contrary) of medical education has had implications for the social and emotional distance necessary for physicians and therapists to treat their patients. An emphasis on diseases, pathology, specific organs, and specific techniques helps create a "separation" that once was quite functional. When there was no anesthesia and death was a common outcome of serious illness and hospitalizations, the conditions and the treatments that occupied physicians' time were of relatively short duration. Because care took less time, this impersonality might also have been of less concern to patients. Though the circumstances that produced this distancing have long since passed, the educative process that brought it about still remains in a time when it is no longer functional. Distance gets in the way of dealing with long-term pain, with chronic loss, and with a dying process that may go on for years.

Medicalization has led to the expansion of medical influence into areas of care where its implications are questionable at best and detrimental at worst. The growth of medicine's influence is a "triumph of the therapeutic." Medicine has taken its place beside law and religion as a major institution of social control—as an arbiter of what is good, important, and valuable in life.[37] In its initial wave of popularity, medicalization was hailed as a reform—a replacement of the mystical and traditional with the objective and the progressive.[38] But in recent years it has been recognized as more of a mixed blessing. Eliot Freidson sounded an early warning: "Medicine is not merely neutral. . . . As applied work it is either deliberately amoral—which is to say, guided by someone else's morality—or it is actively moral by its selective intervention."[39] Other critics have delineated further implications.[40]

The issue of morality is particularly important with respect to the characteristics attributed to illness in general, to chronic illness in particular, and to the "victims" of both. The science from which medicine arose was originally thought to be value-free. It was couched in terms that sought to alleviate guilt, that indicted bacteria rather than individuals as the cause of disease.[41] Thus, while it is probably true that individuals are no longer directly condemned for being sick, the focus of the condemnation has been shifted. Though an individual's character may not be demonstrated in the disease he or she has, it becomes evident in what that person does about it—especially when the problem is chronic.

People who break appointments, fail to follow treatment regimens, or even delay in seeking medical aid are often regarded as possessing many personal flaws. Such people are claimed to be ignorant of the consequences of certain diseases, misinformed as to their symptoms, unable to plan ahead, burdened with shame, guilt, or neurotic tendencies, haunted by traumatic medical experiences, self-abusive in their life-style behaviors (for example, smoking, overeating, sedentary activities), or members of some lower-status religious, ethnic, racial, or socioeconomic group. In short, they appear to be a sorely troubled, if not disreputable, group of people.

This image is ironically reinforced by the depictions of people who have triumphed over adversity and overcome their "handicaps." Such portrayals (on television more than in other media) inevitably emphasize individual qualities of courage and perseverance as the keys to success.[42] The triumph in some single major achievement (the individual walks again, flies a plane, gives a concert performance, plays in professional sports) may be the personal equivalent of the single-intervention medical miracle. But the latter emphasis masks what chronic conditions are all about. The lives of people with disabilities and the adaptations they must make do not center on one dramatic activity or physical achievement, but on many routine, mundane, and complex ones.[43] Emphasis on individual qualities perpetuates a classic blame-the-victim scenario.[44] If they fail to *overcome* their chronic conditions and disabilities, it is *their* problem, *their* personality flaw, *their* weakness.

The argument need not rest at this level of analysis, for it is not clear that the issues of morality and individual responsibility have been fully banished from the etiological search. The concepts of stress and of psychosomatic illness and the growing concern with life-style behaviors in public health bring people, *not* bacteria, to center stage and lead to a reexamination of individuals' roles in their own demise, disability, and even recovery.

The phenomenon of "blaming the individual" need not be confined to professional concepts and their degree of acceptance, for it is reinforced in beliefs of the ordinary citizen. Most surveys have reported that individuals asked the cause of their diabetes, heart attack, cancer, or other diseases or disabilities respond with the scientific language. Yet when the investigator asks: "Why did you get X now?" or "Of all the people in your community, family, etc. who were exposed to X, why did you get it?" then the rational scientific veneer is pierced, and the concern with personal and moral responsibility

101

emerges strikingly. Indeed, the issue "Why me?" becomes of great concern and is generally expressed in moral terms of what they did wrong, blaming carelessness, negligence, or even stupidity in their own behavior. About catching a cold, for example, someone might say: "Well, you know sometimes when your mother says, 'Wrap up and be careful or you'll catch a cold,' well, I didn't."

The moral rhetoric of illness is seen further in societal attempts to control and eliminate many chronic conditions. Thus U.S. society is engaged in "wars" against heart disease, against mental illness, against cancer, against stroke, against birth defects. With society raging against such "killer" diseases, demanding their "unconditional surrender," should it be a surprise that some of the anger at the diseases spills over onto the bearers of the diseases? To some, those with physical and mental disabilities become objects, the permanent reminders of a lost or losing struggle, the symbols of a past and continuing failure. America likes winners. It forgets, denies, rejects, and neglects losers.[45]

When health becomes a paramount value in society and the promotion of that value (the prevention, diagnosis, and treatment of illness) has been monopolized by a specific group, that group is in a position to exercise great control over what people should and should not do to attain that paramount value. Therein lies great danger, for the labels "health" and "illness" have the remarkable ability to de-politicize an issue. Locating the source and the treatment of problems in an individual effectively closes other levels of intervention such as the social or political.[46] The very labeling of a condition as an illness or a medical problem defines it as an undesirable state, something to be controlled or eliminated. The issue becomes not whether to deal with it, but how and when. The debate becomes focused on the degree of sickness or the extent of the health risk involved, and the more perplexing moral issues are obfuscated, if not lost sight of entirely.

This is seen most concretely in the reification of medical measure-ment, where quantification is confused with reality, particularly with regard to the beginning and the end of life. Although frequently people rely on their own values rather than on science to define the beginning of life, even scientists do not agree on when life begins. Nor will earlier detection methods tell what *should* be done in the presence of potential congenital abnormalities.[47]

The same is true of death. New technological advances have led to demands for new definitions of death and for new life-extending technologies (such as organ transplants). Medicalization continues to be used as a way of trying to decide when a life should be ended.

Court rulings have recognized the right of patients to refuse medical care. A current case in Massachusetts seeks to extend this right of refusal by arguing that artificial feeding is "no different from other forms of (medical) life-sustaining treatments such as respirators."[48] That we can measure or sustain certain physiological capacities will neither tell nor prove that an individual is still "alive." Measurement can only be a tool, never an answer to what are ultimately moral and political decisions, not scientific ones.

The medicalization of life processes takes its ultimate toll in our very entry into and departure from this life. Both of these processes have become seriously attenuated in modern society. Both have shifted from the home to the hospital, from being community events to being medical events, and from being largely self-controlled activities to being controlled by experts. As a result, the skills and supports needed to deal with both events are lost or changed. The rituals to mark them are foreshortened, if not disappearing. There are, of course, movements—the home birth and the hospice—that now attempt to redress this balance, but even these are increasingly co-opted: birth rooms and hospices now exist in or within the grounds of hospitals.[49] As David Morgan has noted, the location of such facilities within hospital grounds and organizations may already decide the issue of control.[50]

A reaction to both the technicalization and the medicalization of care is a push toward at-home service—a movement with many ramifications. To talk of self-care and the removal of services to the home as a revolution is something of a misnomer. For most of recorded history the home was the preferred site for the delivery and receipt of health care.[51] It was only in the middle of the twentieth century that a centralization of formal medical care in the hospital, the medical center, and the doctor's office began to take such hold that physicians' home visits virtually disappeared.[52] Self-care, however, though few statistics are available, has never really disappeared.[53]

The push for more out-of-hospital care is multifaceted and recent. There is a growing recognition that chronic illness and disability have become the major health problems of the latter half of the twentieth century. Consequently the treatments themselves, while becoming more palliative (aspirin for arthritis) and adaptive (insulin for diabetes), are at the same time long term and administered regularly by "patients" and their families in their homes.

Another, more strident reaction against the technicalization and medicalization of care is often spearheaded by the women's movement but joined by millions of others in support of deinstitutionalization and the self-help movement.[54] Both movements were fueled by the new economic concern of the 1980s with the finiteness of all resources and with what many perceived as the dangerously rising costs of health care.[55] The answer was cost containment, with diagnosis-related groups (DRGs) as the lever to cut inpatient services and limit hospital stays. All such concerns are compatible with the past decade's questioning of the general efficacy of modern medical care and of the notion that there is any positive connection between higher health care expenditures and better health for the general population.[56]

This period has also seen a series of critiques of almost every form of long-term institutional care, be it in mental hospitals, chronic-disease hospitals, or nursing homes. A recent, systematic study by Tim Booth of old-age homes in the United Kingdom may be the ultimate in such investigations. It makes for very depressing reading. On the one hand, Booth found real differences in what happens to residents: in some homes they die sooner and deteriorate faster than in others. On the other hand, success or failure appeared to have *nothing* to do with how the homes were run or with the caring routines and practices followed by staff. Booth reluctantly concluded that institutionalization tended "to produce a similar press toward routinization and control which is the foundation for the orderly management of homes" and that "the only sure way of limiting its harmful effects is to stop admitting people who, given the chance, could manage with other kinds of support."[57] While systematic data are lacking, the organizational concerns of similar institutions providing long-term care in the United States, whether for those with chronic diseases or disabilities or for those who are simply aging with no place to go, would lead to the expectation of similar results. The familiar refrain "There's no place like home" may thus, for a variety of reasons, become the theme of choice for the delivery and receipt of long-term care.

It will not, however, be entirely the same home from which the shift to the hospital originally took place. Technology has made the home a friendlier environment for procedures previously thought possible only in the hospital under close medical supervision.[58] Examples include improved sanitary and sterile conditions, electrical power for motors to run a variety of machines and fail-safe measures (back-up generators) when power fails, easy access to public and private transportation and to information and professional advice, and surveillance and telemonitoring systems to monitor patients' conditions and regimens.[59] While these advances make more complex technical procedures possible, they can make the home seem more like a private hospital room and thereby defeat the very purpose of the shift.

Though some manufacturers welcome the home health care revolution and see it opening new markets, a European study notes considerable resistance on the part of providers and some serious structural constraints. In 1984 McKinsey and Company surveyed the diffusion of six advanced home therapies (hemodialysis, continuous ambulatory peritoneal dialysis [CAPD], parenteral nutrition, antibiotic therapy, oxygen therapy, and chemotherapy) in ten countries (Belgium, Finland, France, Germany, Italy, the Netherlands, Norway, Sweden, Switzerland, and the United Kingdom). They noted the following:

• Wide variations existed in reimbursement among the countries and among the therapies surveyed. Attitudes toward reimbursement seemed more favorable for older technologies than for newer ones.

• Home therapies were perceived to have negative financial implications for physicians, hospitals, pharmacists, and even patients (in terms of reimbursement and expenses).

• In many countries, laws prohibit home care of patients by specialists and the provision of hospital services at home.

• In most countries an active proinstitutional provider system and concomitant financing not only tended to limit options to hospital treatment but also made it more difficult for the potential home care patient to take advantage of new home therapies.[60]

Some American studies indicate that similar resistances and structural constraints exist.[61]

The general public has long been in favor of home health care. A National Service Corporation Survey of 1,000 consumers reports that "home health care tops the list of alternative health care services they say they need" and "two-thirds want more health care services in their communities."[62] How popular they will remain will depend on how the services are delivered and who delivers them. The most cogent and detailed analysis of the first question has been provided in a series of papers and studies by Gerben DeJong.[63] He contrasts two models of in-home assistance: the agency-directed model of home health services and the self-directed model of attendant services. Figure 5–1 describes this contrast as it exists in three states with home assistance programs.

In their most traditional form, agency-directed home health services are intended to meet a person's episodic acute care needs during posthospital convalescence. The model has, however, been extended to the elderly client with a chronic condition. The service

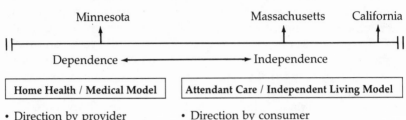

FIGURE 5–1
Continuum of Attendant Care Programs

Home Health / Medical Model	Attendant Care / Independent Living Model
• Direction by provider	• Direction by consumer
• Physician plan of treatment	• No physician plan of treatment
• Nurse supervision	• No nurse supervision
• Aide recruited by agency	• Attendant recruited by consumer
• Payment to provider	• Payment to consumer to provider
• Physician accountable	• Consumer accountable
• Patient role	• Consumer role
• Acute condition	• Chronic condition
• Restorative / episodic care	• Maintenance / continuous care
• "Health care" benefit	• "Social service" benefit

Source: DeJong and Wenker, "Attendant Care," pp. 161–62.

recipient is a patient whose care requires a nurse's supervision in accord with a physician's plan of treatment. Thus, as in the medical model, accountability is assumed to attach to the physician. Payment is made to the home health agency, which, in turn, pays its employees—nurses and nurses' aides. Home health services are viewed as an extension of the health care system and, accordingly, as a health care benefit. The home health model is part of the Medicare and Medicaid programs.[64]

In their most common form, self-directed attendant services are intended to meet a person's continuous chronic care needs. The service user is a consumer who is capable of supervising his or her own care. Thus, as in the independent living model, accountability is assumed to belong to the consumer, not to the physician. Payment is made to the consumer, who, in turn, pays his or her attendants. Attendant services are viewed as an extension of the social services system and thus as a social service or personal maintenance benefit. Unlike home health services, attendant services are not funded by any one agency.

Similar advantages of a self-directed model of care have been found for end-stage renal disease. Here, studies seem to show that those in control of their services not only do better in the long run but, in the face of such an unpredictable disease and technology, also feel more in control and better about themselves.[65] As in the study of advanced home therapies, here, too, there is considerable resistance by providers to the self-directed model. In this instance, however, it is reinforced by attitudes of paternalism, preoccupation with account-ability, and a quest for professionalism.

While the previous discussion outlines the concerns raised by introduction of formal care into the home, the vast majority of such care is more informal.

One of the more comforting findings of recent research into the living situation of our elderly population is that the vast majority are by no means isolated and that only a very small percentage are in long-term care institutions.[66] The problem is that in destroying one myth another may inadvertently be perpetuated. When speaking of people in need, the research continually refers to care being provided by "the family" or "children." The terms themselves imply the sharing of some responsibilities. The empirical data tell another story. Dee A. Jones and Norman J. Vetter conclude that caring does not seem to involve a large network of informal or formal care givers.[67] For whether it be in Europe or New Zealand or this country, the primary care giver in more than 70 percent of all instances is a woman working largely alone.[68] Moreover, she may not be a blood relative of the person she is caring for, and in at least two studies, more than 40 percent of these care givers would themselves be defined as "elderly"—that is, over the age of sixty-five. Interestingly, when the care giving is shared with others, it is not likely to be the most personal care such as washing and dressing, and when males are the primary care givers, this is even more likely to be true.

It is ironic that at a time when statistics point to an ever-growing number of people in need and when pressures and preferences are growing to supply this need in the home, the very group most involved in providing such informal care is under personal and soci-etal pressure to enter and stay in the job market. They are accurately described as "women in the middle," juggling responsibilities for their own families with caring for aged parents (not necessarily their own) and paid employment.[69] As Janice Gibeau has noted, such modern women now have three full-time jobs.[70] Their sense of filial obligation goes deep, and, frankly, they see no alternative. Free time, relaxation, socialization, and pursuit of personal interests are second-ary.

What of the future? Aside from the strain this must put on these women and on their personal relationships, future demographics make the continuation of such a pattern unlikely. Many of these people have reported why they, rather than other siblings, took over the care-giving responsibilities; implied in such data is that at some point there were a number of siblings to choose from. With the post–World War II baby boom past and no new one immediately forecast, American families continue to shrink. With emphasis on geographic mobility in our society, families live farther and farther apart. With greater pressure for women to contribute more to family income, the jobs with flexible hours and working conditions (and usually lower wages with little vertical mobility) so essential to these care givers will necessarily become less desirable. And, finally, the fact that one of every two marriages ends in divorce will necessarily attenuate the ties of women to their in-laws. Though "burnout" may not be imminent for those currently giving care, it is easy to see that there will be a future social burnout—a diminishing available supply of female care givers.

For many reasons, an increasing shift to out-of-hospital care is a good, necessary, and even inevitable phenomenon. It must, however, be acknowledged that for some the shift will come too late. Some families will already be so depleted of energy and resources that they simply will not be ready to try again. For some the attendant risk and responsibility will be too great, while for others there will be no available family.[71]

The shift of care to the home thus involves far more than a mere physical shift in the location of services. Families have to be trained and supported in their efforts to cope with new responsibilities and risks.[72] Whatever the services, they must enhance the independence and control of the recipient.

Finally, there is the further feminization of care giving, which may turn out to be an adjunct to the feminization of poverty. That women retain the overwhelming responsibility for such care will be good neither for them nor for society.

Toward a Unifying Agenda:
A Change in Identity and in Perspective

The United States is a nation in which achievement is deemed more important than birthright, where "all men are created equal," and where society is free of inherited aristocracy. People, however, carry with them the "baggage" of previous generations. The founders had their own notion of equality and equity that at times excluded people with the ascribed characteristics of race or gender. Although it has taken two hundred years to begin to include such people within the rights and privileges of the rest of society, toward the end of the twentieth century American society is beginning to recognize the existence of two other groups whose biophysiological qualities have also excluded them from full participation and whose civil rights have greatly been denied—people who are aging and people with disabilities.

Medicine has long viewed all these groups (women, nonwhites, those who are aging, and people with disabilities) as "less thans," as physiologically inferior and as diseased and vulnerable. These attitudes have been perpetuated in part by what has been at the root of much of modern medicine's success with many acute and infectious diseases—its discovery of the variations among different states of human suffering and the attendant emphasis on differential diagnosis and specific etiologies and treatments. The successes of medical research spread until the medical model as reality and metaphor began to permeate the rest of society—what some have referred to as medicalization. But this model of separation and difference became true not only of medical research, diagnosis, and treatment but also of broader health research and social services. As a result, the recognition of each new disease or medical problem brought with it new specialties, service organizations, public and voluntary associations, and, eventually, national or federal agencies and institutions.

By the mid-twentieth century, though such forces were then (and still are) in full swing, some beginning doubts were being voiced within the medical establishment. Some were concerned about overspecialization, some were concerned about the fragmentation of services, and others were concerned about the lack of continuity in services. A need for more comprehensive, even holistic, approaches was recognized.

This was not merely a humanitarian voice speaking these concerns. Within medicine some wondered whether the bacteriological, specific etiological model had run its course and whether chronic diseases were more multicausal and complex in nature. One of the most articulate and influential of these inquirers was Hans Selye.[73] In pointing out the restrictiveness of our notions of clinical entity, Selye noted that differential diagnosis is based on a very small number of characteristics peculiar to that disease and to no other, and that by far the largest number of signs and symptoms of any disease are shared with a wide variety of disorders and physiological malfunctions. But old ideas die hard, and so research, policy, and clinical services still tend to be more specific than general, more categorical than noncategorical.

What has been true of the professionals who treat "problems" came to be true of people who are being treated. Dominated and controlled by this medical perspective, they, too, often felt that they *were* their diseases, and that their diseases were not like other diseases. They were thus weakened and disempowered when they could least afford it. People often organized along single disease or disability lines, which has too often proved to be a mistake both therapeutically and politically. Therapeutically, it has led them into a no-win game of trying to find others with exactly the same experience with whom to share their problems. Since no one's problems really are the same as someone else's, this has led to an emphasis on differences rather than on similarities. Politically, each "disease group" has had to fight for its own piece of the pie, to portray its disease as more tragic and more deserving than some other, to try to gain a specific privilege for itself, and thus to ignore the common disenfranchisement and oppression of all groups.

A first step in overcoming these misrepresentations is to recognize similarities rather than differences. I call it identifying partial membership but common identity. Segments of society tend to assign negative stereotypes to individuals who possess any characteristics deemed undesirable. Such characteristics can be race, religion, ethnicity, sex, or sexual preference. More recently, they have included health status. Individuals diagnosed as having cancer or heart disease, for example, *become*, in the eyes of the world and too often in their own, their cancer or disease. But as people have multiple roles, so they can have multiple identities. The French language distinguishes many qualities by whether the verb is *"être"* or *"avoir,"* "to be" or "to have." So, too, it can be with one's disabilities; people can have them without being them. The disability and the person remain separate.

Efforts at building coalitions among those with multiple identities have a checkered history.[74] But I am not as pessimistic as Robert Binstock that bridges across the communities of those with disability and those who age cannot be built.[75] A recent Harris poll telephone survey of a thousand people with disabilities is quite instructive in this regard. Because it is so new and so important, it is worth discussing in some detail.[76] (Some of the survey results are included in the appendix to this chapter.) While it documents many interesting facts of limitations on activity and discrimination, it also, for the first time (to my knowledge), gathered data on issues of identity.

Although nearly 85 percent of the sample had a "moderate" to "very severe" disability, only 43 percent considered themselves disabled. Those who held jobs were more likely to reject the label disabled. Mary Jane Owen may well be right in interpreting this tendency as due to their awareness that to become eligible for most assistance or benefits to deal with whatever added difficulties they face because of their particular limitations, they would have to officially declare and document themselves as unemployable! They are therefore pressured to disassociate themselves from the concept of "handicapped" in order to retain the self-image of "employable."[77]

This lack of full self-identification, however, did not prevent them from identifying with other people with disabilities. Only 16 percent had no such feeling, while an overwhelming majority of nearly 75 percent said that they felt at least some sense of common identity with other disabled people, and 40 percent felt it somewhat or very strongly. Surprisingly, the strength of the identification varied little with age or the duration or severity of disability.

A plurality of those surveyed extended this sense of identification to other minority groups. Forty-five percent of all people with a disability felt they were a minority group in the same sense that blacks and Hispanics are, while 42 percent felt that they were not, and 12 percent were not sure or refused to answer the question. Significantly, the younger they were and the earlier the onset of their limitation, the more likely they were to share such an identity. Equally significant, those over sixty-five were less sure of their answers or were more apt to refuse to answer the questions about identity than those in the youngest age group (sixteen to thirty-four).

A near consensus emerges on how disability should be treated under the law. Three of every four people with a disability believe that civil rights laws that protect minorities against discrimination should also protect those with a disability; only 17 percent disagree. As Mary Jane Owen points out,

> This agreement with the concept of classifying "the handicapped" as a minority is surprisingly high and illustrates that, in spite of the negative stereotypes and "second-class" status of disability, there is an emerging impression that *other* disabled people, with whom a very large majority (84 percent) feels some attachment, constitute a minority class of citizens. This idea is strongest among younger people so one might expect greater group identification to develop in the years ahead.[78]

Consistent with such a view is the overwhelming support for greater private and governmental effort to educate, train, rehabilitate, provide equipment for, and help adapt the environments of those who can work. Support is also stated for increasing, at least somewhat, government and private benefits for those who cannot work.

TABLE 5–1

PERFORMANCE LIMITATIONS OFTEN ASSOCIATED
WITH SELECTED CONDITIONS

Selected Conditions	Difficulty interpreting or processing information	Severe or complete loss of sight or hearing	Poor balance	Speech or communication problems
Alzheimer's disease	X		X	X
Cerebral palsy			X	X
Heart disease				
Multiple sclerosis	X	X	X	X
Normal aging	X	X	X	
Parkinson's disease	X		X	X
Rheumatoid arthritis				
Spinal cord injury	X		X	X
Stroke, cerebral trauma	X	X	X	X
Visual impairment		X	X	
Hearing impairment		X	X	X
Pregnancy			X	
Short stature				
Obesity			X	

Performance (column group header)

Thus, it seems that increasing segments of the population, young as well as old, with disabilities see themselves in the same boat.[79] With these changes, the influence of special interests may break down. While recognizing that choices must be made and priorities set, groups perceiving their similar needs and dilemmas may be able to reason together and set more joint agendas for action.[80]

A parallel step would be to seek out common service, design, and policy needs. The first common interest is in society's notions of health and illness, disability and aging. The United States is a death-denying, age-denying, and disability-denying society. Whatever else this denial does, it negates the possibility of accumulating resources (material, psychological, and social) to deal with the inevitable and ubiquitous disabilities we all will face in daily living. With several

TABLE 5–1 (continued)

Limitations

Limitations of stamina or strength	Difficulty reaching	Loss of upper extremity skills	Loss of coordination	Difficulty handling or fingering	Difficulty bending and kneeling	Reliance on walking aids	Inability to use lower extremities
X	X	X	X	X	X	X	X
X						X	X
X	X		X		X	X	X
X	X				X	X	
X	X	X	X	X	X	X	X
X	X	X	X	X	X	X	X
X	X	X	X	X	X	X	X
X	X	X	X	X	X	X	X
X	X				X		
	X						
X					X		

SOURCE: Orleans and Orleans, "High and Low Technology—Sustaining Life at Home," pp. 358–59.

others, I share the conviction that it is impossible to create a society without disease and disability.[81] This does not mean that I am against prevention or attempts to alleviate human pain and suffering (though, with Illich, I am concerned about any attempt to eliminate them entirely),[82] but rather that such efforts must be placed in perspective. Perfect health or life without disability or limitations is not an attainable goal. Like Tocqueville, I do not seek to deny the existence of biophysical differences; I merely wish to create a society in which their existence does not predetermine the fullness of one's participation and appreciation.

This chapter has pointed to the near universality and the multi-

TABLE 5–2
Design Implications of Performance Limitations

Design Implications	Difficulty interpreting or processing information	Severe or complete loss of sight or hearing	Poor balance	Speech or communication problems
Early warning devices: smoke detectors, visual/auditory warning, emergency response system	X	X		X
Efficient layout with attention to closely related activities				
Reduction in background noise	X	X	X	X
Reduction of glare: gradual changes in light intensity		X	X	
Control manipulation not dependent upon fine motor coordination: door/window hardware, faucet controls, light switches, thermostats				
Decreased force to operate and use: doors and windows, appliances, furnishings, equipment			X	
Protection against falls and supports to maintain balance: provide stair railings, minimize thresholds, eliminate tripping hazards, install nonslip flooring		X	X	
Eliminate need for extensive reaching: adjustable shelves, cabinets, clothes rods			X	

TABLE 5–2 (continued)

Limitations

Limitations of stamina or strength	Loss of upper extremity skills	Loss of coordination	Difficulty handling or fingering	Difficulty bending and kneeling	Reliance on walking aids	Inability to use lower extremities
	X	X	X		X	X
X	X	X		X	X	X
	X	X	X	X		X
X	X	X	X	X	X	X
X	X	X	X	X	X	X
X	X	X	X	X	X	X

SOURCE: Orleans and Orleans, "High and Low Technology—Sustaining Life at Home," pp. 360–61.

ple and changing nature of disability across the age continuum. Thus, statistical normality, at least, does not consist of the absence of "chronic problems" but rather of their presence. In an insightful paper, Miriam Orleans and Peter Orleans have translated these notions into service design issues.[83] They advocate the elimination of "special user" groups, each of which requires specialized designs to solve its particular problem. There are, in fact, a myriad of problems that are spread across life styles. Loss of stamina and energy, disorientation, and memory loss are conditions experienced by many. Building on the work of E. Steinfeld and L. Hiatt, they have developed a list of common performance limitations that are characteristic of a large number of chronic health problems or disabilities across all age groups.[84] As seen in table 5–1, such limitations are commonly caused by large numbers of conditions.

Building again on the work of Steinfeld and Hiatt, Orleans and Orleans have shown (table 5–2) how appropriate design technology can help ameliorate performance limitations commonly associated with these conditions. They conclude: "Our success in modifying the environment will determine whether many of us, when . . . we experience . . . disabilities or deficits, can live independently."[85]

Extending the concept of the universality of need to the general population and throughout the life cycle should help resolve a current dilemma plaguing many services—the rejection of needed services because, in declaring need, people also have to identify themselves as fragile or diseased, in short, stigmatized.[86] As a recent issue of *Disability Rag* has noted in another context, the humiliation rituals associated with tort claims (such as postponing rehabilitation and declaring oneself totally disabled) deprive many not only of their rights but also of their just entitlements.[87]

What can be done for the design of services can easily be done for other programs. In Sweden 2000 has been chosen as the year when "mutual care [will] be an important part of people's everyday lives."[88] Some of the changes likely to emerge will be different notions about extended families and appropriate living arrangements; the integration of care-giving responsibilities (with respite care, leaves, flextime for both sexes); agencies with more comprehensive, socially oriented, and consumer-responsive services, and providers that are less exclusively technical, professional, and agency-directed.[89]

These changes, of course, must be part of an even larger effort to change attitudes toward and the structure of care giving in our society.[90] Scott Osberg and his colleagues, reflecting on an expanded definition of disability, concluded,

We must come to understand that environmental factors are not merely at the periphery of our involvement as health care professionals. Nor should we consider ourselves powerless in coping with environmental barriers. In fact, our status as health care professionals often provides us with the clout needed to help force the service delivery system into providing needed adaptations for our patients. But even more to the point, we ourselves constitute a large portion of the patient's environment that may at times require alteration and adaptation—in our behaviors and in our institutions of health care delivery.[91]

In short, it is not someone else's problem, it is ours—maybe not ours today, but certainly ours tomorrow.

Appendix: Disabled Americans' Self-Perceptions

TABLE A–1

A PROFILE OF THE SAMPLE OF 1,000 DISABLED AMERICANS,
BY KEY MEASURES OF DISABILITY

	Percentage of Sample
Type of Disability[a]	
Physical disability	44
Nonparalytic orthopedic impairments	29
Neuromotor/neuromuscular disorders	8
Brain dysfunction/memory loss/senility	6
Other physical disabilities	2
Sensory impairment	13
Blind/visual impairment	7
Hearing, speech, language	6
Mental disability	6
Mental retardation/developmental disabilities	3
Mental illness	3
Other serious health impairments	32
Heart disease/blood or blood vessel disease	16
Respiratory or pulmonary disease	5
Cancer/diabetes/kidney disease/other disease	11
Not sure/refused to answer	4
Multiply disabled	32
Not multiply disabled	68

(Table continues)

117

TABLE A–1 (continued)

	Percentage of Sample
Onset of limitation	
Birth to adolescence	13
Young adult	21
Middle age	22
After age 55	37
Limitation of activities	
Cannot work, keep house, etc.	46
Limited in amount or kind of work	38
Other activities limited	8
Not limited at all	7
Severity of disability	
Slight	14
Moderate	31
Somewhat severe	28
Very severe	24
Respondent considers self disabled[b]	
Yes	43
No	54
Not sure/refused to answer	3

NOTE: Detail may not add to totals because of rounding.
a. Most limiting condition or single condition.
b. Based on 828 designated respondents *only.*
SOURCE: Louis Harris and Associates, *Disabled Americans' Self Perceptions: Bringing Disabled Americans into the Mainstream,* Study no. 854009 (New York: International Center for the Disabled, 1986), p. 19.

TABLE A-2
PERCEPTIONS OF HOW FEDERAL LAWS HAVE HELPED DISABLED PEOPLE

Q.: Since the late 1960s, the federal government has passed laws to give better opportunities to disabled and handicapped Americans. How much do you think these laws have helped disabled Americans—have they helped a great deal, somewhat, not too much, or hardly helped at all?

	No. of Respondents	*Distribution of Answers (percent)*				
		A great deal	Some- what	Not too much	Hardly at all	Not sure/ refused to answer
Age						
16–34 years	190	15	48	19	12	5
35–44 years	136	14	52	13	17	4
45–54 years	145	17	45	19	9	11
55–64 years	232	24	47	15	6	7
65 and over	296	29	42	9	9	11
Onset of limitation						
Birth–adolescence	139	21	48	19	6	7
Young adult	226	14	46	14	19	7
Middle age	216	19	46	18	8	8
After age 55	336	29	43	11	8	9
Limitation of activities						
Cannot work, keep house, etc.	445	23	42	14	12	8
Limited in amount or kind of work	381	22	48	14	9	7
Other activities limited	86	20	49	15	6	10
Not limited at all	77	17	58	14	4	7
Severity of disability						
Slight	144	25	49	14	6	7
Moderate	310	21	51	12	8	8
Somewhat severe	284	21	47	15	10	8
Very severe	237	22	39	16	14	8
Total	1,000	22	46	14	10	8

NOTE: Detail may not add to totals because of rounding.
SOURCE: Same as table A-1, p. 21.

TABLE A–3
SHOULD ANTIDISCRIMINATION LAWS COVER DISABLED PEOPLE?

Q.: Do you think that the civil rights laws that cover minorities against discrimination should also cover disabled persons, or not?

		Distribution of Answers (percent)		
	No. of Respondents	Should cover	Should not cover	Not sure/ refused to answer
Age				
16–34 years	190	82	14	4
35–44 years	136	83	11	6
45–54 years	145	77	17	6
55–64 years	232	72	21	8
65 and over	296	68	18	14
Onset of limitation				
Birth–adolescence	139	86	10	4
Young adult	226	77	17	5
Middle age	216	73	20	7
After age 55	336	71	16	13
Limitation of activities				
Cannot work, keep house, etc.	455	75	15	10
Limited in amount or kind of work	381	73	19	7
Other activities limited	86	79	12	10
Not limited at all	77	72	23	5
Severity of disability				
Slight	144	74	19	7
Moderate	310	78	15	7
Somewhat severe	284	72	19	9
Very severe	237	75	15	10
Total	1,000	75	17	9

NOTE: Detail may not add to totals because of rounding.
SOURCE: Same as table A–1, p. 22.

TABLE A–4
Do Disabled People Share a Feeling of Common Identity?

Q.: To what extent do you feel that you have a sense of common identity with other disabled people—do you feel that you have no sense of common identity, some sense of common identity, a somewhat strong sense of common identity, or a very strong sense of common identity?

	No. of Respondents	No sense	Some sense	Somewhat strong sense	Very strong sense	Not sure/ refused to answer
Age						
16–34 years	190	18	39	24	18	1
35–44 years	136	16	45	16	21	2
45–54 years	145	14	32	22	23	8
55–64 years	232	15	34	22	22	8
65 and over	296	18	29	16	19	19
Onset of limitation						
Birth-adolescence	139	11	41	22	23	3
Young adult	226	14	40	20	19	7
Middle age	216	11	33	27	22	7
After age 55	336	20	30	15	20	15
Limitation of activities						
Cannot work, keep house, etc.	455	14	31	17	23	14
Limited in amount or kind of work	381	17	36	23	20	5
Other activities limited	86	15	45	18	12	10
Not limited at all	77	31	32	15	16	6
Severity of disability						
Slight	144	25	41	18	11	5
Moderate	310	20	33	19	18	11
Somewhat severe	284	12	39	25	19	5
Very severe	237	12	27	15	30	15
Total	1,000	16	34	20	20	10

Distribution of Answers (percent)

NOTE: Detail may not add to totals because of rounding.
SOURCE: Same as table A–1, p. 45.

121

TABLE A–5
Do Disabled Persons Constitute a Minority Group?

Q.: Do you feel that disabled persons are a minority group in the same sense that Blacks and Hispanics are, or not?

	No. of Respondents	Distribution of Answers (percent)		
		Are a minority group	Are not a minority group	Not sure/ refused to answer
Age				
16–34 years	190	54	40	5
35–44 years	136	53	44	3
45–54 years	145	48	41	12
55–64 yeyars	232	45	43	13
65 and over	296	37	43	20
Onset of limitation				
Birth-adolescence	139	56	35	9
Young adult	226	49	43	8
Middle age	216	40	48	12
After age 55	336	43	39	19
Limitation of activities				
Cannot work, keep house, etc.	455	43	40	17
Limited in amount or kind of work	381	47	43	9
Other activities limited	86	45	45	10
Not limited at all	77	48	50	2
Severity of disability				
Slight	144	40	52	8
Moderate	310	48	41	11
Somewhat severe	284	45	45	10
Very severe	237	47	36	17
Total	1,000	45	42	12

NOTE: Detail may not add to totals because of rounding.
SOURCE: Same as table A–1, p. 46.

Notes

1. Secretariat for Future Studies, Sweden, *Care and Welfare at the Crossroads* (Stockholm, 1982), p. 4.

2. See, for example, Lee Sechrest, "Social Science and Social Policy: Will Our Numbers Ever Be Good Enough?" in R. L. Schottland and M. M. Maine, eds., *Social Science and Social Policy* (New York: Sage, 1985), pp. 63–91; Harriet McBryde Johnson, "Who Is Handicapped? Defining the Protected Class under the Employment Provisions of Title V of the Rehabilitation Act of 1973," *Review of Public Personnel Administration*, vol. 2 (1981), pp. 49–61; Lawrence Haber, "Trends and Demographic Studies on Programs for Disabled Persons," in Leonard G. Perlman and Gary F. Austin, eds., *Social Influences in Rehabilitation Planning: Blueprint for the Twenty-first Century*, A Report of the Ninth Mary E. Switzer Memorial Seminar (Alexandria, Va.: National Rehabilitation Association, 1985), pp. 27–37; and Frank Bowe, *Demography and Disability: A Chartbook for Rehabilitation* (Hot Springs: Arkansas Rehabilitation Research and Training Center, 1983).

3. Frank Bowe, *Disabled Adults in America* (Washington, D.C.: President's Committee on Employment of the Handicapped, 1984); and Frank Bowe, *U.S. Census and Disabled Adults: The Fifty States and the District of Columbia* (Hot Springs: Arkansas Rehabilitation Research and Training Center, 1984).

4. National Center for Health Services, *National Health Survey* (Washington, D.C.: Department of Health and Human Services, 1982), Series 10, no. 146; and Office of Technology Assessment, Congress of the United States, *Technology and Handicapped People* (Washington, D.C.: Office of Technology Assessment, 1982), p. 11.

5. David Pfeiffer, "The Number of Disabled Persons in the U.S. and Its Policy Implications" (Paper presented to the Society for the Study of Chronic Illness, Impairment, and Disability at Reno, Nevada, April 23–26, 1986).

6. Alain Colvez and Madeleine Blanchet, "Disability Trends in the United States Population, 1966–76: Analysis of Reported Causes," *American Journal of Public Health*, vol. 71, no. 5 (May 1981), pp. 464–71.

7. Ronald W. Wilson and Thomas F. Drury, "Interpreting Trends in Illness and Disability," *Annual Review of Public Health*, vol. 5 (1984), pp. 83–106.

8. K. Liu, K. Manton, and W. Alliston, "Demographic and Epidemiologic Determinants of Expenditures," in R. L. Vogel and H. C. Palmer, eds., *Long-Term Care: Perspectives from Research and Demonstration* (Washington, D.C.: U.S. Government Printing Office, 1983).

9. Patrice Hirsch Feinstein, Marian Gornick, and Jay N. Greenberg, "The Need for New Approaches in Long-Term Care," in Patrice Hirsch Feinstein, Marian Gornick, and Jay N. Greenberg, eds., *Long-Term Care Financing and Delivery Systems: Exploring Some Alternatives*, Conference Proceedings, January 24, 1984, Washington, D.C. (Health Care Financing Administration, Publication no. 03174, June 1984).

10. Paul W. Newacheck, Peter P. Budetti, and Neal Halfon, "Trends in Activity-limiting Chronic Conditions among Children," *American Journal of Public Health*, vol. 76, no. 2 (February 1986), pp. 178–83.

11. Robert J. Haggerty, K. J. Roghmann, and I. B. Pless, *Child Health and the Community* (New York: John Wiley, 1975).

12. Newacheck, Budetti, and Halfon, "Trends in Activity-limiting Chronic Conditions."

13. Melvin Levine, "The High Prevalence–Low Severity Disorders of School Children," *Advances in Pediatrics*, vol. 29 (1982), pp. 530–54; Katarina Michelson, Roger Byring, and Prijo Bjorkgmen, "Ten-Year Follow-up of Adolescent Dyslexics," *Journal of Adolescent Health Care*, vol. 6 (1985), pp. 31–34; and Howard Adelman, Linda Taylor, and Perry Nelson, "Prevalence and Treatment of Learning Problems in Upper and Lower Income Areas," *American Journal of OrthoPsychiatry*, vol. 52, no. 4 (1982), pp. 719–23.

14. René Dubos, *The Mirage of Health* (Garden City, N.Y.: Anchor, 1961), flyleaf.

15. Harry H. Gordon, "Perspectives on Neonatology—1980," in Albert R. Jonsen and Michael J. Garland, eds., *Ethics of Newborn Intensive Care* (Berkeley, Calif.: Health Policy Program and Institute of Government Studies, University of California, 1976); Earl E. Shelp, "Evolution of a Subspecialty," in *Born to Die: Deciding the Fate of Critically Ill Newborns* (New York: Free Press, 1986), pp. 78–88; Adrienne Asch, "On the Question of Baby Doe," *Health/PAC Bulletin*, vol. 16, no. 6 (August 1986), pp. 6, 8–10; and Barbara Katz Rothman, "On the Question of Baby Doe," *Health/PAC Bulletin*, vol. 16, no. 6 (August 1986), pp. 7, 11–13.

16. Elizabeth Kubler-Ross, *On Death and Dying* (New York: Macmillan, 1969); Elizabeth Kubler-Ross, *Death: The Final Stage of Growth* (Englewood Cliffs, N.J.: Prentice-Hall, 1975); Robert J. Lifton, *Six Lives–Six Deaths* (New Haven, Conn.: Yale University Press, 1979); and Richard Kalish, *Death, Grief, and Caring Relationships* (Monterey, Calif.: Brooks/Cole, 1981).

17. James F. Fries, "Aging, Natural Death, and the Compression of Morbidity," *New England Journal of Medicine*, vol. 303 (1980), pp. 130–35.

18. Jan E. Blanpain, guest ed., "Advanced Technology and Health Care in the Home," *International Journal of Technology Assessment in Health Care*, vol. 1, no. 2 (1985), pp. 271–393; and Blanpain, "The Changing Environment of Health Care," ibid., p. 273.

19. Nancy A. Brooks and Ronald R. Matson, "Coping: Adapting the Basics to Your Own Personal Situation," *M.S. Patient Service News*, vol. 23, no. 1 (Spring 1982), pp. 1, 4.

20. Uta Gerhardt and Marianne Brieskorn-Zinke, "The Normalization of Hemodialysis at Home," in Julius Roth and Sheryl Burt Ruzek, eds., *The Adoption and Social Consequences of Medical Technologies*, vol. 4 of *Research in the Sociology of Health Care—A Research Annual* (Greenwich, Conn.: JAI Press, 1986), pp. 271–317.

21. Dennis C. Turk and Marjorie A. Speers, "Diabetes Mellitus: A Cognitive-Functional Analysis of Stress," in Thomas G. Burish and Lawrence A. Bradley, eds., *Coping with Chronic Disease* (New York: Academic Press, 1983).

22. Ivan Illich, *Medical Nemesis* (New York: Pantheon, 1976); and Roberta J. Apfel and Susan M. Fisher, *To Do No Harm: DES and the Dilemmas of Modern Medicine* (New Haven, Conn.: Yale University Press, 1984).

23. Lauro S. Halstead and David Wiechers, *Late Effects of Poliomyelitis* (New

York: Symposia Foundation, 1985); and Gini Laurie and Judith Raymond, eds., *Proceedings of Rehabilitation Gazette's Second International Post-Polio Conference and Symposium on Living Independently with Severe Disability* (St. Louis, Mo.: Gazette International Networking Institute, 1984).

24. May Clarke, *Trouble with Feet*, Occasional Papers on Social Administration, no. 29 (London: G. Bell & Sons, 1969); and Irving Kenneth Zola, "The Mirage of Health Revisited: On the Omnipresence of Illness," in *Socio-Medical Inquiries* (Philadelphia: Temple University Press, 1983), pp. 135–50.

25. Richard K. Scotch, *From Good Will to Civil Rights: Transforming Federal Disability Policy* (Philadelphia: Temple University Press, 1984).

26. Harlan Hahn, "Disability Policy and the Problem of Discrimination," *American Behavioral Scientist*, vol. 28 (1985), pp. 293–318; and Deborah Stone, *The Disabled State* (Philadelphia: Temple University Press, 1984).

27. Erik H. Erikson, *Childhood and Society* (New York: Macmillan, 1963); Carol Gilligan, *In a Different Voice: Psychological Theory and Women's Development* (Cambridge, Mass.: Harvard University Press, 1982); L. Kohlberg, "Continuities in Childhood and Adult Moral Development Revisited," in Paul Baltes and K. Warner Schaie, eds., *Life-Span Developmental Psychology: Personality and Socialization* (New York: Academic Press, 1973), pp. 179–204; L. Kohlberg, "Stages and Aging in Moral Development—Some Speculation," in *Gerontologist*, vol. 13, no. 4 (1973), pp. 497–502; Daniel Levinson et al., *The Seasons of a Man's Life* (New York: Knopf, 1978); and Gail Sheehy, *Passages: Predictable Crises of Adult Life* (New York: E. P. Dutton, 1976).

28. Ken Dychtwald, "Consumer Behavior: Speculations on the Future of Aging, Wellness, and Self-Care," in Clement Bezold, Jerome A. Halperin, Howard L. Binkley, and Richard A. Ashbaugh, eds., *Pharmacy in the Twenty-first Century—Planning for an Uncertain Future* (Va.: Institute for Alternative Futures and Project HOPE, 1985), pp. 67–78.

29. Roth and Ruzek, *The Adoption and Social Consequences of Medical Technologies.*

30. Susan Bell, "A New Model of Medical Technology Development: A Case Study of DES," in Roth and Ruzek, *The Adoption and Social Consequences of Medical Technologies*, pp. 1–32; and John Ost and Phillip Antweiler, "The Social Impact of High-Cost Medical Technology: Issues and Conflicts Surrounding the Decision to Adopt CAT Scanners," ibid., pp. 33–92.

31. Gregory L. Dixon and Alexandra Enders, *Low-Cost Approaches to Technology and Disability* (Washington, D.C.: D:ATA Institute, 1984); Office of Technology Assessment, *Technology and Handicapped People* (New York: Springer, 1983); Alexandra Enders, "Questionable Devices," Proceedings of the Second International Conference on Rehabilitation Engineering, Ottawa, Ontario, 1984, pp. 271–76; and Alexandra Enders, "Issues and Options in Technology for Disability," in Carroll L. Estes, Constance W. Mahoney, and Judith H. Heumann, eds., *Toward a Unified Agenda* (San Francisco: Institute for Health and Aging, University of California, San Francisco, 1986), pp. 64–89.

32. Robert A. Bernstein, "Backward Thinking about Disability," *New York Times*, February 8, 1986.

33. Thomas S. Szasz and Marc C. Hollender, "A Contribution to the Phi-

losophy of Medicine: The Basic Models of the Doctor-Patient Relationship in Its Historical Context," *American Journal of Psychiatry,* vol. 115 (December 1958), pp. 522–28.

34. Gerhardt and Brieskorn-Zinke, "The Normalization of Hemodialysis at Home."

35. Nancy M. Crewe, Irving Kenneth Zola, and Associates, *Independent Living for Physically Disabled People* (San Francisco: Jossey-Bass Publishers, 1983); and Gerben DeJong, "Defining and Implementing the Independent Living Concept," ibid., pp. 4–28.

36. Anita Diamont, "Bedside Manners: Of Doctors, Patient Abuse, and Regulation," *Boston Phoenix,* November 10, 1981, Lifestyle section.

37. Irving Kenneth Zola, "Medicine as an Institution of Social Control," *Sociological Review,* vol. 20, no. 4 (November 1972), pp. 487–504; Peter Conrad and Joseph W. Schneider, *Deviance and Medicalization: From Badness to Sickness* (St. Louis, Mo.: C. V. Mosby, 1980); and Eliot Freidson, *Profession of Medicine* (New York: Dodd-Mead, 1970).

38. Barbara Wooton, *Social Science and Social Pathology* (London: Allen and Unwin, 1959).

39. Freidson, *Profession of Medicine,* p. 346.

40. Thomas Szasz, *The Myth of Mental Illness: Foundations of a Theory of Personal Conduct* (New York: Hoeber-Harper, 1961); Thomas Szasz, *Law, Liberty, and Psychiatry* (New York: Macmillan, 1963); and Irving Kenneth Zola, "In the Name of Health and Illness: On Some Socio-Political Consequences of Medical Influence," *Social Science and Medicine,* vol. 9 (February 1975), pp. 83–87.

41. Talcott Parsons, "Social Structure and Dynamic Process: The Case of Modern Medical Practice," chapter 10 in *Social System* (Glencoe, Ill.: Free Press, 1951), pp. 428–79.

42. Irving Kenneth Zola, "Depictions of Disability: Metaphor, Message, and Medium in the Media," *Social Science Journal,* vol. 22, no. 4 (October 1986), pp. 5–17.

43. Joseph Schneider and Peter Conrad, *Having Epilepsy: The Experience and Control of Illness* (Philadelphia: Temple University Press, 1983); Gerhardt and Brieskorn-Zinke, "The Normalization of Hemodialysis at Home"; and Irving Kenneth Zola, *Missing Pieces: A Chronicle of Living with a Disability* (Philadelphia: Temple University Press, 1982).

44. William Ryan, *Blaming the Victim* (New York: Pantheon, 1970).

45. This claim has often been made in regard to our Vietnam veterans and is one that some post-polio survivors in the throes of the post-polio syndrome have made about many health authorities.

46. Robert Crawford, "You Are Dangerous to Your Health: The Ideology of Politics of Victim Blaming," *International Journal of Health Services,* vol. 7 (1977), pp. 663–80; and Robert Crawford, "Individual Responsibility and Health Politics," in Susan Reverby and David Rosner, eds., *Health Care in America: Essays in Social History* (Philadelphia: Temple University Press, 1979).

47. Barbara Katz Rothman, *The Tentative Pregnancy: Prenatal Diagnosis and the Future of Motherhood* (New York: Viking, 1986); and Neil A. Holtzman,

"Screening for Congenital Abnormalities," *International Journal of Technology Assessment in Health Care,* vol. 1, no. 4 (1985), pp. 805–19.

48. Peter Mancusi, "Supreme Judicial Court Is Asked to Halt Comatose Patient's Feedings," *Boston Globe,* May 8, 1986, pp. 27, 33.

49. Boston Women's Health Book Collective, *The New Our Bodies, Ourselves* (New York: Simon & Schuster, 1985); Margaret Gold, *Life Support: What Families Say of Hospitals, Hospice, and Home Care for the Fatally Ill* (Mt. Vernon, N.Y.: Institute for Consumer Policy Research, Consumers Union Foundation, 1983).

50. David L. Morgan, "Failing Health and the Desire for Independence: Two Conflicting Aspects of Health Care in Old Age," *Social Problems,* vol. 30 (October 1982), pp. 40–50.

51. Blanpain, "The Changing Environment."

52. Count D. Gibson and Bernard M. Kramer, "Site of Care in Medical Practice," *Medical Care,* vol. 3 (January–March 1965), pp. 14–17.

53. Office of Health Economics, *Without Prescription—A Study of the Role of Self-Medicalization,* no. 27 (London: Office of Health Economics, 1968); and Karen Dunnell and Ann Cartwright, *Medicine Takers, Prescribers, and Hoarders* (London: Routledge and Kegan Paul, 1972).

54. Boston Women's Health Book Collective, *The New Our Bodies, Ourselves;* Phil Brown, *The Transfer of Care: Psychiatric Deinstitutionalization and Its Aftermath* (London: Routledge and Kegan Paul, 1985); Wolf Wolfensberger, *The Principle of Normalization in Human Services* (Toronto, Ontario: National Institute on Mental Retardation, 1972); Irving Kenneth Zola, "Helping One Another: A Speculative History of the Self-Help Movement," *Archives of Physical Medicine and Rehabilitation,* vol. 60, no. 10 (October 1979), pp. 452–56; and A. H. Katz and E. I. Bender, "Self-Help Groups in Western Society—History and Prospects," *Journal of Applied Behavioral Science,* vol. 12 (1976), pp. 265–82.

55. Brian Abel-Smith, "Value for Money in Health Services," *Social Security Bulletin,* vol. 37 (1974), pp. 17–28; and John B. McKinlay and Sonia M. McKinlay, "The Questionable Contribution of Medical Measures to the Decline of Mortality in the United States in the Twentieth Century," *Milbank Memorial Fund Quarterly/Health and Society,* vol. 55 (1977), pp. 405–528.

56. Tim Booth, *Home Truths—Old People's Homes and the Outcome of Care* (Brookfield, Vt.: Gower, 1986).

57. Ibid., pp. 207, 209.

58. A partial list of such procedures culled from Blanpain, "Advanced Technology," includes home hemodialysis, continuous ambulatory peritoneal dialysis, home peritoneal nutrition, home antibiotic therapy, home oxygen therapy, continuous chemotherapy, insulin pump therapy, bone stimulation therapy, and heart function therapy.

59. Kitty Dawson and Andrew Feinberg, "Hospitals in the Home," *Venture* (August 1984), pp. 38–43.

60. Blanpain, "The Changing Environment."

61. Alonzo Plough, *Borrowed Time: Artificial Organs and the Politics of Extending Lives* (Philadelphia: Temple University Press, 1986).

62. Walter J. McNerney, "The Rationale for Siting Advanced Health Tech-

nologies at Home," in Blanpain, "Advanced Technology,"p. 287.

63. Gerben DeJong, *The Need for Personal Care Services by Severely Physically Disabled Citizens in Massachusetts,* Personal Care and Disability Study, Report no. 1 (Waltham, Mass.: Brandeis University, Levinson Policy Institute, April 1977); Gerben DeJong, *Meeting the Personal Care Needs of Severely Physically Disabled Citizens of Massachusetts,* Personal Care and Disability Study, Report no. 2 (Waltham, Mass.: Brandeis University, Levinson Policy Institute, October 1977); Gerben DeJong, "Needs of Disabled Persons: In-Home Attendant Services," in *Toward a Unified Agenda,* pp. 46–56; and Gerben DeJong and Teg Wenker, "Attendant Care," in Crewe and Zola, *Independent Living for Physically Disabled People,* pp. 157–70.

64. DeJong, "Needs of Disabled Persons."

65. Gerhardt and Brieskorn-Zinke, "The Normalization of Hemodialysis"; Nancy Kutner and Donna Brogan, "Disability Labeling vs. Rehabilitation Rhetoric for the Chronically Ill: A Case Study in Policy Contradictions," *Journal of Applied Behavioral Science,* vol. 21, no. 2 (1985), pp. 169–83; and R. G. Simmons, C. Anderson, and L. Kamstra, "Comparison of Quality of Life of Patients on Continuous Ambulatory Peritoneal Dialysis, Hemodialysis, and after Transplantation," *American Journal of Kidney Disease,* vol. 4 (1984), pp. 253–55.

66. Marjorie H. Cantor, "The Family: A Basic Source of Long-Term Care for the Elderly," in Feinstein, Gornick, and Greenberg, *Long-Term Care,* pp. 107–12.

67. Dee A. Jones and Norman J. Vetter, "A Survey of Those Who Care for the Elderly at Home: Their Problems and Their Needs," *Social Science and Medicine,* vol. 19, no. 5 (1984), pp. 511–14.

68. Laura Reif and Branna Trager, eds., *International Perspectives on Long-Term Care* (New York: Haworth Press, 1985); Avery Jack, "Who Cares for the Dependent Disabled" (Paper presented to the New Zealand Association Conference, October 1985); and Susan A. Stephens and Jon B. Christianson, *Informal Care of the Elderly* (Lexington, Mass.: Lexington Books, 1986).

69. Elaine M. Brody, "Women in the Middle and Family Help to Older People," *Gerontologist,* vol. 21, no. 5 (1981), pp. 471–80; Elaine M. Brody, "Parent Care as a Normative Family Stress," *Gerontologist,* vol. 25, no. 1 (1985), pp. 19–29; Marjorie H. Cantor, "Strain among Caregivers: A Study of Experience in the United States," *Gerontologist,* vol. 23, no. 6 (1983), pp. 597–604; Neena L. Chappell, "Social Support and the Receipt of Home Care Services," *Gerontologist,* vol. 25, no. 1 (1985); and Amy Horowitz and Rose Dobrof, *The Role of Families in Providing Long-Term Care to the Frail and Chronically Ill Elderly Living in the Community,* Final Report to the Health Care Financing Administration, Grant 18-P-97541/2-02 (New York: Brookdale Center on Aging of Hunter College, 1982).

70. Janice L. Gibeau, "Breadwinners and Caregivers: Working Patterns of Women Working Full-Time and Caring for Dependent Elderly Family Members" (Ph.D. diss., Florence Heller Graduate School, Brandeis University, 1986).

71. Cantor, "The Family"; Gerhardt and Brieskorn-Zinke, "The Normaliza-

tion of Hemodialysis"; and Norbert H. Lameire, "Experience with CAPD as Home Dialysis," in Blanpain, "Advanced Technology," pp. 305–13.

72. Jean Hermesse, "Cost-Effective Health Technology at Home as an Avenue for Reducing National Health Expenditures—A View from Government," in Blanpain, "Advanced Technology," pp. 289–306.

73. Hans Selye, *The Stress of Life* (New York: McGraw-Hill, 1956).

74. Renee R. Anspach, "From Stigma to Identity Politics: Political Activism among the Physically Disabled and Former Mental Patients," *Social Science and Medicine*, vol. 13 A, no. 6 (1979), pp. 765–73; and Arlene Feinblatt, "Political Activism among Physically Disabled Individuals," *Archives of Physical Medicine and Rehabilitation*, vol. 62 (August 1981), pp. 360–64.

75. Robert H. Binstock, "Aging and Rehabilitation: The Birth of a Social Movement" (Paper presented as a conference summary at Aging and Rehabilitation: A National Conference on the State-of-the-Art, Washington, D.C., December 2, 1984).

76. Louis Harris and Associates, *Disabled Americans' Self Perceptions: Bringing Disabled Americans into the Mainstream,* Study no. 854009 (New York: International Center for the Disabled, 1986).

77. Mary Jane Owen, "Who Are These Disabled People and What Do They Want?" *Update* (National Organization on Disability), April 28, 1986.

78. Ibid.

79. Judith Rodin, "Aging and Health: Effects of the Sense of Control," *Science*, vol. 233 (September 19, 1986), pp. 1271–76.

80. Kathleen Kautzer, "A Review of Scholarly Literature on the Theme of Empowerment," unpublished manuscript, Florence Heller Graduate School, Brandeis University, 1984.

81. Clyde J. Behney, "Technology and Disability: Policy Issues in the Year 2005" (Paper presented at Marketplace Problems in Communications Technology for Disabled People, Washington, D.C., February 20–21, 1986); and Dubos, *Mirage of Health.*

82. Illich, *Medical Nemesis.*

83. Miriam Orleans and Peter Orleans, "High and Low Technology—Sustaining Life at Home," in Blanpain, "Advanced Technology," pp. 353–63.

84. E. Steinfeld and L. Hiatt, *Multiple Disabilities through the Lifespan* (Washington, D.C.: Architectural and Transportation Barriers Compliance Board, 1983), pp. 1.3–1.7.

85. Orleans and Orleans, "High and Low Technology," p. 356.

86. Suzanne Rie Day, "Use of Congregate Services by the Elderly in Subsidized Housing," Final report to the Gerontological Society of America, Washington, D.C., and the New Jersey Division on Aging, Department of Community Affairs, Trenton, N.J., August 1985.

87. "Insult to Injury," *Disability Rag* (May/June 1986), pp. 1–8.

88. Secretariat for Future Studies, *Care and Welfare*, pp. 40–41.

89. Rothman, *The Tentative Pregnancy;* Joanne Unruh, "Beyond the Professions—A Study of Community Involvement in the Lives of Multi Handicapped Children" (Ph.D. diss., Union Graduate School, 1982); Gordon F. Streib, Edward Folts, and Mary Anne Hilker, *Old Homes–New Families, Shared*

Living for the Elderly (New York: Columbia University Press, 1984); Walter N. Leutz, Jay N. Greenberg, Ruby Abrahams, Jeffrey Prottas, Larry M. Diamond, and Leonard Gruenberg, *Changing Health Care for an Aging Society—Planning for the Social Health Maintenance Organization* (Lexington, Mass.: Lexington Books, 1985); Crewe and Zola, *Independent Living for Physically Disabled People;* and DeJong, "Needs of Disabled Persons."

90. Irving Kenneth Zola, "The Medicalization of Aging and Disability: Problems and Prospects," in *Toward a Unified Agenda,* pp. 20–40.

91. Scott Osberg, Paul J. Corcoran, Gerben DeJong, and Elaine Ostroff, "Environmental Barriers and the Neurologically Impaired Patient," *Seminars in Neurology,* vol. 3, no. 2 (June 1983), pp. 180–94.

6
The Treatment of Women under Medicare

Shelah Leader

Although Medicare has fulfilled one of its major purposes by ensuring access to hospital services for the nation's elderly, it suffers from two critical design flaws. First, Medicare does not protect its beneficiaries from heavy direct costs for medical goods and services, placing the burden of those direct costs most heavily on those who are least able to afford it. Second, although women constitute some 60 percent of Medicare's enrollees, the program's design does not suit the specific financial and health care needs of women. Rather, Medicare is based on a traditional medical model that reflects a male pattern of health care use. Women receive proportionately fewer benefits under Medicare and experience greater liability and gaps in coverage.

These flaws are being exacerbated by two significant trends: increased reliance on ambulatory care in response to prospective payment for hospital inpatient services and the demographic trend toward an increasingly aged, female, and frail population. Increased age is associated with chronic illness and declining average gross income. The oldest old are the most likely to be at or near the poverty level. This paper explores the effects on women aged sixty-five and older of the dynamic interaction between Medicare's design flaws and these trends.

Costs to Beneficiaries

Medicare requires substantial cost sharing by beneficiaries, and these costs have been rapidly rising. In 1985, beneficiaries spent almost $10 billion to meet Medicare's cost-sharing requirements, or 70 percent more than in 1981. The Part A (hospital) deductible was $492 in 1986

The views expressed in this chapter are solely those of the author and do not reflect the position of the American Association of Retired Persons.

and would have risen to $572 in 1987 had not Congress agreed to hold it to $520. As it was, the deductible rose 38 percent between 1984 and 1986.

The 1987 annual premium for Part B (medical) coverage is $214.80; it has risen 131 percent since 1977. In addition, beneficiaries must pay an annual $75 Part B deductible before Medicare will begin to help defray covered medical costs for physicians' visits.

Furthermore, in 1986 beneficiaries paid $2.8 billion in claims for nonassigned physicians' bills. The total amount of money charged by physicians above Medicare's allowed fee increased 100 percent from 1980 to 1986.

Out-of-pocket costs to beneficiaries for noncovered services and products have risen sharply in the past decade. In 1984, for example, out-of-pocket expenses for these noncovered services totaled nearly $332 per capita.[1] Stated differently, consumers directly paid for 60 percent of the cost of uncovered items such as dental and vision care, prescriptions, and medical equipment and supplies.[2]

Furthermore, the elderly and their families directly pay for 50 percent of the total cost of nursing home care at an average annual cost of about $20,000 per elderly institutionalized member.

In sum, Medicare pays for less than half of the total health care costs of the elderly, and the bulk of Medicare expenditures are for acute care in hospitals. Sixty-nine percent of Medicare funds pay for hospital care, and three-fourths of all payments for hospital services to the elderly come from Medicare. In contrast, Medicare beneficiaries directly pay for about 25 percent of the total health care costs they incur but pay for only 3 percent of the total cost of hospital care.

Medicare has not significantly reduced the financial liability of the elderly for health care. What it has achieved is a shift in the composition of that burden. Since Medicare does pay most of the cost associated with hospital stays, the elderly primarily pay for nursing home care, physicians' services, and noncovered goods and services such as prescription drugs and vision, dental, and preventive care. And, as the site of service delivery shifts from the hospital ward to outpatient departments and physicians' offices, beneficiaries are exposed to further Part B liability.

Cataract surgery, for example, is one of the leading procedures performed on Medicare beneficiaries. An estimated 1.2 million people underwent this procedure in 1985 at a total cost of $3.5 billion.[3] In 1981, a three-day hospital stay was normal for this surgical procedure; by 1985, 70 percent of the procedures were done in a hospital outpatient setting.

The inspector general recently concluded that "the outpatient

TABLE 6–1

Out-of-Pocket Expenses (Excluding Premiums) as a
Percentage of Income (in 1981 Dollars), by Income Group

Income Level	Percentage of Aged Persons	Out-of-Pocket Expenses as Percentage of Income
Poor/near poor (less than 1.25 × poverty level)	26	14.1
Low income (1.25 to less than 2 × poverty level)	24	4.3
Middle income (2 to less than 4 × poverty level)	30	2.4
High income (more than 4 × poverty level)	20	1.4

Source: Adapted from U.S. Congress, Senate, Special Committee on Aging, *Medicare and the Health Costs of Older Americans: The Extent and Effects of Cost Sharing*, Washington, D.C., 1984, pp. 26, 27.

department of the hospital is the most expensive place to have cataract surgery if the hospital collects coinsurance."[4]

Specifically, a beneficiary's liability could be as high as $2,500 when the hospital copayment is collected, the physician does not accept assignment, and the patient does not have private supplemental insurance.[5] The assignment rate in 1983 for outpatient cataract surgery was only 50.5 percent.[6] Although Congress reduced Medicare payments for cataract surgery in the 1986 Budget Reconciliation Act, other ambulatory surgical procedures continue to generate heavy costs for beneficiaries. The burden of cost sharing falls most heavily on those with limited incomes. Specifically, cost sharing is far heavier for the poor and near-poor than it is for middle- and high-income groups (see table 6–1). This is so, in part, because the poor and near-poor are far less likely than other income groups to be covered by private supplemental health insurance. And since only about a quarter of them are eligible for both Medicare and Medicaid, they are more likely than higher-income groups to be covered only by Medicare.[7]

Data from the 1977 National Medical Care Expenditure Survey indicate that poor and near-poor persons with only Medicare coverage are primarily female (62.6 percent), are older (50.2 percent are age seventy-five and older), and tend not to be married and living with a spouse.[8] Recent census data confirm that aged women have higher poverty rates than men (15.6 percent compared with 8.5 percent for men).[9] This group of female beneficiaries is most burdened by Medicare's cost-sharing requirements and limited benefits. To understand why, we need to explore gender differences in use of services and Medicare expenditures.

Utilization Patterns

Hospitals. Medicare was intentionally designed to emphasize payment for hospital care because available data in the 1960s showed that the aged were sicker, poorer, and less likely to have private health insurance than the population as a whole. And insured aged persons received reimbursement for only a quarter of their total hospital expenses.[10]

Once Medicare was enacted, hospitalization rates among the elderly increased dramatically and have remained higher than they are for the general population. This pattern is well established, but within the elderly population there is a clear and persistent gender difference in the incidence of hospitalization, in rates of use, and in costs.[11] Men are more likely to use only hospital services, while women are more likely to need posthospital and skilled nursing facilities.[12] These different needs may be due to the fact that older men tend to be married and are nursed by their wives, whereas older women tend to be widowed. (Eighty percent of elderly men are married, compared with 40 percent of women.)[13] Another contributing factor may be the higher number of very old women who are hospitalized. Advanced age prolongs the recuperative process. The point is that although posthospital services are available under Medicare, qualifying for them is extremely difficult.[14] Under existing Medicare rules, for example, beneficiaries must have been hospitalized for at least three days before entering a skilled nursing facility (SNF). But prospective payment for inpatient hospital care has led to across-the-board reductions in the average length of stays in hospitals, and technological innovation has shifted the site of many procedures to the outpatient department. Consequently, it has become increasingly difficult for beneficiaries to satisfy the three-day hospital stay requirement for admission to an SNF.

Aged men have both higher rates of hospital use than women and higher Medicare reimbursement for hospital care, although women receive more days of care (see tables 6–2 and 6–3).

Physicians. Perhaps because women suffer from more long-term chronic diseases than men, they see physicians more frequently.[15] Although disability increases with age in both men and women, older women have a higher incidence of disability than older men.

TABLE 6–2
HOSPITAL DISCHARGE RATE PER 1,000 PERSONS
FOR ALL LISTED PROCEDURES, 1984

Sex and Age	Total Discharges (millions)	Rate per 1,000	Total Days of Care (millions)	Average Length of Stay
All 65+	11,226	400.4	100,237	8.9
Male 65+	4,799	424.8	42,454	8.8
Female 65+	6,427	383.9	57,783	9.0

SOURCE: U.S. Department of Health and Human Services, Public Health Service, *Utilization of Short-Stay Hospitals, United States, 1984, Annual Summary,* PHS 86-1745, March 1986, p. 14.

Surprisingly, although women have higher rates of visits to doctors, Medicare reimbursements for physicians' services are consistently higher for men.[16] Women's greater number of visits may be offset by the higher cost of visits by men. The higher cost for men may be due to a combination of factors: more visits may occur in hospitals, treatment may be for surgery or grave illness, or the physician may be a specialist. All of these factors are associated with higher fees.

Drugs. The elderly as a group are heavy users of prescription drugs; 75 percent of them received at least one prescription in 1977, compared with 58 percent of the total population. And the annual average number of prescribed medicines per user was 14.2—twice that of the total population.[17]

Medicare's exclusion of self-administered prescription drugs burdens women more than men because women are issued more prescriptions than men. Women are more frequent users of drugs, have higher rates of use, and have higher out-of-pocket expenses for drugs. Since lower-income persons tend to have higher drug expenses, lower-income women are disproportionately burdened by high direct costs for essential drugs.[18] A leading example of how women are disproportionately harmed by Medicare's bias toward acute-care coverage and exclusion of prescription drugs concerns elderly persons suffering from heart disease. Diseases of the circulatory system in general are extremely prevalent among the aged and are a leading cause of hospitalization. Yet, for valid medical reasons, most of the coronary artery bypass procedures are performed on men, while most of the drugs used to treat cardiovascular disease are prescribed to women.[19] Men who are surgically treated for heart disease have most of their costs borne by Medicare. But women who manage their

135

TABLE 6–3

Persons Served and Average Reimbursement per Enrollee in Medicare Part A and Part B (Estimated), 1984

Type of Service	All Persons		Men		Women	
	No. served per 1,000 enrollees	Average reimbursement per enrollee (dollars)	No. served per 1,000 enrollees	Average reimbursement per enrollee (dollars)	No. served per 1,000 enrollees	Average reimbursement per enrollee (dollars)
Total Part A	239.6	1,233	246.9	1,329	234.7	1,168
Inpatient	228.5	1,159	238.1	1,267	222.0	1,086
SNF	10.7	17	8.3	13	12.3	20
Home health	51.6	56	45.0	49	56.0	62
Total Part B	698.9	599	665.8	634	720.8	576
Physician and other medical services	677.3	494	643.7	524	699.5	474
Outpatient	326.7	104	314.0	109	335.1	101
Home health	0.9	1	0.5	1	1.1	1

Source: Unpublished data, U.S. Department of Health and Human Services, Health Care Financing Administration, Division of Program Statistics.

condition with expensive drugs receive no reimbursement; although they may have the same medical condition, because they receive different treatment, they receive different coverage.

This financial burden on beneficiaries is exacerbated by continuing large increases in the prices of prescription drugs. The Bureau of Labor Statistics indicates that between 1981 and the first half of 1985 the inflation rate for drugs was 56 percent, compared with an overall rise in the consumer price index of 23 percent during that time.[20] In addition, because older women rely heavily on social security, which is indexed to general inflation, as their primary source of income, they are less able to afford uncontrolled price increases for prescription drugs. Medicare simply does not meet their needs.

Another way of looking at the differential benefits Medicare provides to men and women is to examine the pattern of program outlays for covered goods and services.

Expenditure Patterns

We have seen that older men use proportionately more hospital services, while women use more physicians' and post–acute care services as well as prescription drugs. This pattern of use has significant consequences with respect to personal liability for the cost of services and the distribution of Medicare funds.

First, as previously noted, the bulk of Medicare expenditures is for hospital care. Nearly 70 percent of Medicare funds pay for hospital services, while about one-fourth are for physicians' services.[21]

Second, Medicare's deductibles and coinsurance for Part A services make up only 30 percent of total Part A expenditures, while personal liability under Part B equals 69 percent of the total cost. In 1980 about 80 percent of all enrollees experienced some cost sharing under Part B.[22]

Another way of stating this is that in 1984 Medicare paid for 75 percent of the total cost per capita of hospital care but for only 58 percent of physicians' costs.[23] We have already seen that out-of-pocket costs per capita constitute only 3 percent of total hospital costs but 26 percent of the costs of physicians' services.[24]

Simply stated, more money is spent per capita on male enrollees than on women. In 1984, the average total Medicare reimbursement for men was $1,831 compared with $1,744 for women.[25] This pattern of greater expenditures on behalf of men has persisted over time and for each age group. In 1967, Medicare reimbursement per person served and per person enrolled was higher for men.[26] Expenditure data from 1976 provide further evidence of this pattern (see table 6–4).

TABLE 6–4
MEDICARE REIMBURSEMENT PER ENROLLEE, 1976
(dollars)

Age	Total	Men	Women
67–68	518	578	471
69–70	555	613	511
71–72	603	674	551
73–74	657	717	613
75–79	736	793	699
80–84	818	854	798
85+	866	937	832

SOURCE: Victor Fuchs, "Though Much Is Taken: Reflections on Aging, Health, and Medical Care," *Milbank Memorial Fund Quarterly*, vol. 62, no. 2 (Spring 1984), p. 151.

And the most recent Medicare data confirm this pattern (see table 6–3).[27]

Chronic Care

Medicare's structure of benefits is not only less satisfactory for meeting the medical needs of older women; it also fails to address their need for sub-acute care. Medicare's exclusion of chronic care services in the home or in institutions places a far greater burden on women than it does on men. Indeed, the gap in coverage for chronic care is a true financial and personal catastrophe for older women.

Demographic trends indicate rapid growth in the numbers of Medicare beneficiaries most vulnerable to uncontrolled costs for health care. Persons age eighty-five and older now constitute about 10 percent of the elderly, but that age group is increasing the most rapidly and is expected to constitute 15 percent of the aged population by the year 2000. About 70 percent of those eighty-five and older are women,[28] whose incomes are lower than those of men their age and of the elderly in general.[29] Furthermore, very old women are at greatest risk of institutionalization in nursing homes and the concomitant crushing expense. Projections indicate significant growth in the nursing home population by the year 2040.[30] As long as Medicare continues to exclude from coverage care provided in intermediate care facilities and as long as private nursing home insurance is largely unavailable, the cost of care provided in nursing homes will be borne primarily by the elderly—principally by widows, many of whom must impoverish themselves to become eligible for the benefits of long-term care under Medicaid.

The evidence supports the conclusion of a study for the American Association of Retired Persons (AARP) done by ICF Incorporated that "on average, single women households will spend a greater share of their incomes for out-of-pocket expenditures than single men or married couple households."[31]

Costs to beneficiaries can also be measured in terms of lost earnings or the hidden value of free services. There is strong evidence that women disproportionately bear the cost of supplementing or replacing Medicare home health benefits. Under current law, Medicare provides very limited home health benefits for post-acute illness to the homebound on an intermittent or part-time basis. Medicare does not cover home care for the chronically ill and frail or for the disabled. A recent study by the National Center for Health Services Research in the U.S. Department of Health and Human Services found that women provide more than 70 percent of the free care given to noninstitutionalized disabled elderly persons. About one-third of the care givers are age sixty-five and older. And most of those dependent on free care are women.[32]

Again, the need for home care services is exacerbated by efforts to contain hospital costs. Many who formerly recuperated in hospitals must fend for themselves at home. While there is general recognition that something must be done to meet the growing need of the frail and chronically ill for long-term care services, there is no consensus on a specific policy solution. It is in this context that we should evaluate proposals to reform Medicare and provide so-called catastrophic coverage.

Astute observers of the Medicare program concluded that "the program has accommodated more the pre-Medicare male pattern than the female pattern of medical care use."[33] The point is accurate but needs to be amplified. Because of Medicare's bias toward comprehensive coverage of inpatient hospital services at the expense of outpatient care, preventive health services, and basic necessities such as drugs, eyeglasses, dentures, and hearing aids, aged women have proportionately fewer of their health care needs covered and are exposed to greater financial liability than men. And that liability constitutes a significantly greater burden on women when measured as a percentage of their income. Before Medicare, a hospital stay could pauperize an elderly person. Today women are pauperized by nursing home care and other noncovered services. In fact, the average older woman spends the same percentage of her income for health care that the elderly in general spent before the advent of Medicare.

Any proposal to modify Medicare's benefit structure and cost-sharing requirements should be evaluated in light of the health and financial needs of the majority of program beneficiaries—older women.

Reform Options

Unfortunately, congressional leaders and the administration are unwilling at present to address these real needs of older women. Rather, so-called catastrophic insurance proposals advanced in early 1987 primarily focus on enriching Part A hospital coverage. The leading catastrophic proposals—the Bowen plan and the Stark-Gradison approach—exclude long-term care for the frail and the chronically ill. Because they fail to address the leading source of catastrophic expense for the elderly—nursing home care—these proposals are not in reality catastrophic plans. Furthermore, since out-of-pocket payment for prescription drugs is the second heaviest financial burden on the elderly, exclusion of drugs from proposals to reform Medicare also limits the utility of these proposals.

The current congressional debate is simply focusing on enriching covered benefits under Medicare by capping out-of-pocket payments for covered services. Here again, the exclusion of payments for non-covered goods and services and the caps being discussed—$2,000 or $1,500—are too high to be of real benefit to lower-income beneficiaries, and especially to women.[34] To reach the $1,500 cap, for example, a beneficiary would have to be hospitalized and incur an additional $4,900 in covered charges against which a copayment would be deducted. Yet $600 in out-of-pocket expenses for noncovered goods and services would be a devastating expense for an older person with an income below the median.

Because of the huge budget deficit, Congress and the administration are unwilling to mandate publicly financed comprehensive insurance for long-term care or even to expand Medicare benefits to cover prescription drugs, glasses, hearing aids, and other essential goods and services. In this political climate, the only realistic option available to some older women is to enroll in a health maintenance organization (HMO) or other capitated system. They at least offer protection against large and unpredictable out-of-pocket expenses, and many HMOs offer prescription drugs and other noncovered services. Another option available to a few beneficiaries is to enroll in an experimental "social" HMO, which offers a continuum of care encompassing the services of long-term care.

But these options are not universally available. Only about 4 percent of Medicare beneficiaries have enrolled in capitated systems, and growth projections are modest. The Reagan administration strongly supports capitated systems for Medicare, but its preference for industry self-monitoring and the poor performance by some risk contractors raise grave questions about quality control and consumer protection.

Furthermore, Medicare beneficiaries tend to have strong attachments to their physicians and are generally unwilling to change providers in order to protect themselves financially. There is little evidence, for example, that the elderly have switched to physicians who have signed agreements with Medicare to accept assignment in all cases. The inescapable conclusion is that the elderly are attached to their fee-for-service physicians and do not shop for less costly providers.

What, then, can be done to provide the majority of beneficiaries with meaningful financial protection against the cost of care?

Individual savings are not the answer to the cost of nursing home care. Medical individual retirement accounts (IRAs) would be primarily a tax shelter, not a solution for the vast majority of Americans, for several reasons.[35] And private insurers cannot meet the need for affordable policies because their administrative costs are very high compared with those of Medicare, and they cannot command a large market share. Indeed, the results of initial efforts by groups such as the AARP to market nursing home insurance have been very disappointing.[36] In fact, the elderly can no longer purchase insurance coverage for prescription drugs from AARP—the benefit is simply too expensive to offer.

All of the evidence points to the ultimate need for comprehensive, publicly funded coverage of all services and goods that are medically necessary to maintain health and functioning at the highest possible level. Such a sweeping change, however, can be implemented only after a broad consensus has been created.

In the interim, modest improvements in current benefits and coverage can be achieved. In 1987, for example, Congress may ease access to home health care and skilled nursing facilities (SNFs) by dropping the three-day prior hospitalization requirement for SNF admission, reducing the amount of the SNF copayment, and broadening the eligibility rules for home care. It is also possible that a modest respite care benefit will be adopted as part of a catastrophic bill, along with a very modest prescription drug benefit.

In addition, there is growing support for expanding Medicaid eligibility by mandating a national minimum eligibility standard, broadening the coverage of the medically needy, and enacting a spousal impoverishment provision to ensure a minimum maintenance income for the spouse of an institutionalized person.

These stop-gap measures could provide a little relief to older women and pave the way for future improvements in coverage and benefits. But much more needs to be done to meet the real needs of our most vulnerable elderly.

Conclusion

Experience from other countries such as Canada is persuasive that the surest way to provide access to needed goods and services while maintaining financial protection for individuals is through comprehensive national health insurance financed through income taxes. Canada's experience has shown that including everyone in the risk pool permits health care costs to be controlled.[37]

If, for example, we dramatically expand Medicare coverage by imposing income-related premium surcharges, the cost of premiums will continue to rise uncontrollably without a mechanism to contain or reduce all health care costs. Only a national health insurance plan gives government the power to contain the costs of all health care goods and services, thereby protecting taxpayers and premium payers from cost increases that exceed the general inflation rate. It can achieve this by setting the price for all physicians' services, globally budgeting hospital care, and limiting capital investment. Consequently, health care expenditures per capita and as a percentage of GNP are far lower in Canada than in the United States.

As a limited policy response to a larger public need, Medicare is of limited use to the majority of program beneficiaries. Current proposals to tinker with it around the edges are unlikely to meet the real needs of older women for financial protection and long-term care services.

Notes

1. Daniel Waldo and Helen Lazenby, "Demographic Characteristics and Health Care Use and Expenditures by the Aged in the United States: 1977–1984," *Health Care Financing Review*, vol. 6, no. 1 (Fall 1984), p. 10.

2. Ibid., p. 11.

3. U.S. Congress, House of Representatives, Select Committee on Aging, *Cataract Surgery: Fraud, Waste, and Abuse*, July 19, 1985, p. iii.

4. U.S. Department of Health and Human Services, Office of the Inspector General, *Medicare Cataract Implant Surgery*, March 1986, p. 12.

5. Ibid.

6. Ira Burney and George Scheiber, "Medicare Physicians' Services: The Composition of Spending and Assignment Rates," *Health Care Financing Review*, vol. 7, no. 1 (Fall 1985), p. 94.

7. U.S. Congress, Senate, Special Committee on Aging, *Medicare and the Health Costs of Older Americans: The Extent and Effects of Cost Sharing*, April 1984.

8. Ibid.

9. U.S. Department of Commerce, Bureau of the Census, *Money Income and Poverty Status of Families and Persons in the United States: 1985*, Series P-60, no. 154, p. 27.

10. Theodore Marmor, *The Politics of Medicare* (Chicago: Aldine, 1970), p. 18.

11. Waldo and Lazenby, "Expenditures by the Aged," p. 7.

12. Karen Young and Charles Fisher, "Medicare Episodes of Illness: A Study of Hospitals, Skilled Nursing Facilities, and Home Health Agency Care," *Health Care Financing Review*, vol. 2, no. 2 (Fall 1980), p. 10.

13. U.S. Department of Commerce, Bureau of the Census, *Money Income and Poverty Status of Families and Persons in the United States: 1982*, Series P-60.

14. See, for example, Shelah Leader, *Home Health Benefits under Medicare* (Washington, D.C.: American Association of Retired Persons, Public Policy Institute, 1986).

15. U.S. Department of Health and Human Services, National Center for Health Statistics, *Use of Health Services by Women Sixty-five Years of Age and Over, United States*, Series 13, no. 59, August 1981, p. 3; and *Vital and Health Statistics*, no. 128, January 23, 1987, p. 3.

16. U.S. Department of Health and Human Services, Health Care Financing Administration, *Health Care Financing Program Statistics, Medicare and Medicaid Data Book, 1984*, HCFA Pub. no. 03210, June 1986, p. 37.

17. Waldo and Lazenby, "Expenditures by the Aged," p. 14.

18. U.S. Department of Health and Human Services, National Center for Health Statistics, *Drug Utilization in Office-based Practice, a Summary of Findings*, Series 13, no. 65, March 1982; and U.S. National Health Care Expenditures Study, "Prescribed Medicines: Use, Expenditures, and Sources of Payment," Data Preview 9, April 1982.

19. U.S. Department of Health and Human Services, Food and Drug Administration, *Drug Utilization in the United States—1984*, Sixth Annual Review, March 1986, p. 5.

20. U.S. Congress, Committee on Energy and Commerce, Subcommittee on Health and the Environment, "Price Increases for Prescription Drugs and Related Information," staff report, July 15, 1985.

21. Waldo and Lazenby, "Expenditures by the Aged," p. 11.

22. Marian Gornick, "Options for Change under Medicare," *Health Care Financing Review*, vol. 5, no. 1 (Fall 1983), p. 35.

23. Waldo and Lazenby, "Expenditures by the Aged," p. 11.

24. Ibid.

25. Unpublished data, U.S. Department of Health and Human Services, Health Care Financing Administration, Office of Research, Division of Program Statistics.

26. Henry Brehm and Rodney Coe, *Medical Care of the Aged* (New York: Praeger, 1980), p. 75.

27. Unpublished data, U.S. Department of Health and Human Services, Health Care Financing Administration, Division of Program Statistics. Estimate of 1984 utilization and reimbursement is based on a 5 percent sample.

28. U.S. Department of Commerce, Bureau of the Census, *Population Estimates and Projections*, Series P-25, no. 937, 1983.

29. U.S. Congress, Senate, Special Committee on Aging, *Aging America: Trends and Projections*, 1985–1986 edition, p. 47.

30. Cited ibid., pp. 97–98.

31. ICF Incorporated, *Medicare's Role in Financing the Health Care of Older Women* (Washington, D.C.: ICF, 1985), p. 26.

32. Cited in the *Washington Post*, August 4, 1986.

33. Brehm and Coe, *Medical Care of the Aged*, p. 77.

34. See, for example, Leon Wyszewianski, "Families with Catastrophic Health Care Expenditures," *Health Services Research*, vol. 21, no. 5 (December 1986); and Timothy Smeeding and Lavonne Straub, "Health Care Financing among the Elderly," *Journal of Health Politics, Policy, and Law*, vol. 12, no. 1 (Spring 1987).

35. Proponents of medical IRAs assume that everyone will save the maximum allowable amount every year for at least twenty years and that the compound rate of interest will rapidly increase the amount saved. But inflation in the health care sector far outpaces interest rates and is more than a match for savings accounts. In 1983 only 17 percent of American families had an IRA, and this form of tax-sheltered savings was very strongly correlated with high income (over $50,000 a year). Given the current cost of nursing home care, $100,000 in savings would be exhausted in less than five years of institutionalization.

36. "Survey of Consumer Finances, 1983," *Federal Reserve Bulletin*, September 1984. Private long-term care insurance is projected by ICF, Inc., to save only 8 percent of Medicaid expenditures. See Joshua Wiener et al., "Money, Money, Who's Got the Money?" (Paper presented at the Conference on Health in Aging, State University of New York at Albany, April 18–19, 1986), p. 19.

37. Robert G. Evans, "Health Care in Canada: Patterns of Funding and Regulation," *Journal of Health Politics, Policy, and Law*, vol. 8, no. 1 (Spring 1983), pp. 1–3.

Index of Names

A Note on the Book

This book was edited by
Janet Schilling and Trudy Kaplan of the
Publications Staff of the American Enterprise Institute.
The figures were drawn by Hördur Karlsson.
The text was set in Palatino, a typeface designed by Hermann Zapf.
Coghill Book Typesetting Company, of Richmond, Virginia,
set the type, and Edwards Brothers Incorporated,
of Ann Arbor, Michigan, printed and bound the book,
using permanent, acid-free paper.